RENOIR'S GARDEN

The artist Pierre-Auguste Renoir spent his last years at Les Collettes, near Cagnes-sur-Mer and within sight of the Mediterranean.

Looking for a home in the favourable climate of the south, Renoir fell in love with Les Collettes, where a shimmering meadow surrounded the green-shuttered farmhouse and gnarled olive trees framed spectacular views of the distant mountains and the sea.

In this 'paradise on earth' Renoir set up his easel and painted outdoors, or had flowers, fruit and vegetables brought into his studio. He studied the colours of roses for the flesh tints of his models. The garden was an endless source of inspiration during these fruitful last years when he completed some 600 important paintings and embarked on a form of artistic expression new to him – sculpture.

With its rich blend of photographs of the house and garden today and nostalgic photographs of Renoir at his easel, as well as reproductions of some of his paintings, *Renoir's Garden* is a celebration of the artist's life and work in this sanctuary on the Côte d'Azur. Derek Fell reveals Les Collettes as everything a family garden should be: a place to entertain visitors, an exciting playground for Renoir's younger sons and a source of fresh fruit and vegetables for the table. It also produced crops on a commercial scale.

With an affectionate foreword by the painter's great-grandson Jacques Renoir, this book is a superb evocation of a much loved and hitherto little known garden, now preserved as a living museum to the artist.

RENOIR'S GARDEN

RENOIR'S GARDEN

DEREK FELL

Foreword by Jacques Renoir

FRANCES LINCOLN

FOR RENOIR

Previous pages Renoir's chair, easel and
artist's materials.
Palm seen through olive tree.

Right Self-Portrait with a White Hat
(1910).

Following page Poppies and olive tree.

Frances Lincoln Limited
Apollo Works, 5 Charlton King's Road,
London NW5 2SB

Renoir's Garden
Copyright © Frances Lincoln Limited 1991
Text copyright © Derek Fell 1991
Photographs copyright © Derek Fell 1991

British Library cataloguing in publication
data
Fell, Derek
Renoir's Garden.
1. France. Gardens
I. Title
712.60944

ISBN 0-7112-0698-8

Set in 11/16pt Bodoni in England
by SX Composing Ltd, Rayleigh, Essex
Printed and bound in Hong Kong
1 3 5 7 9 8 6 4 2

CONTENTS

Foreword

by Jacques Renoir

Renoir at his easel in the garden of an apartment he rented next to the post office in Cagnes village, shortly before his move to Les Collettes. The design of the balustrade in the background matches almost exactly a terrace wall built at Les Collettes.

My great-grandfather, Pierre-Auguste Renoir (1841–1919), was known even to his wife simply as 'Renoir' and to Gabrielle, his favourite model, as *Maître*. He was a simple man who lived for his art. He began decorating china at the age of thirteen and died at seventy-eight, painting until the very end. He outlived his wife Aline by four years. She had borne three sons: my grandfather, Pierre, and my great-uncles, Jean and Claude (the youngest, known as Coco, whom Renoir fathered when he was almost sixty).

The last eleven years of his life were spent at Les Collettes, a nine-acre estate overlooking the Mediterranean at Cagnes. Les Collettes was to Renoir what Giverny, in Normandy, was to his friend and fellow Impressionist painter Claude Monet. It was a sanctuary which not only provided subjects for his paintings in his later years, but also gave him a stimulating place to receive visitors.

However, the gardens which Renoir and Monet each created were quite different. Monet planted his garden as an ardent plantsman, using plants like paints on a palette, and was much influenced both by the informal English cottage garden and by Japanese stroll gardens. He cultivated and collected a great many flowers and transformed a site that was neglected and forlorn into his vision of a flowering paradise. Renoir, on the other hand, sought to envelop himself in an aura of peace and tranquillity, to preserve things much as they were, to keep a traditional working farm of ancient olive and orange groves and a market garden, and to grow flowers to paint. At Les Collettes he cherished the old farmhouse both as a symbol of a vanishing way of life and as a landscape feature.

I was born in a house on the hill directly facing Les Collettes, in the shadow of the Château Grimaldi; I spent many happy days in Renoir's home and garden. Best of all, I remember climbing the old olive trees and building a tree house in one of them. Olives were still harvested from the trees, and it was a treat to sprinkle the oil they made on to a sandwich of freshly baked bread filled with lettuce, ham, anchovies and tomatoes.

There were still rabbits and chickens in the grounds, and I played with them. I remember there was also a big fishtank with bright red goldfish. Everywhere were memories of Renoir and his children. I sometimes used Renoir's wheelchair as a go-kart, and recall my delight at finding some of Coco's toys in the basement.

Among the descendants of Renoir who are alive today is Paul Renoir, the son of Coco who was Renoir's youngest child. Paul is an art dealer who spends much of his time in Central America. In 1978, a branch of his side of the family emigrated to Canada and established a water bottling enterprise in Edmonton called 'Renoir Water', with Paul's oldest son, Emanuel Renoir, as president. A younger son, Pierre, returned to France to pursue a career as an artist, specializing in drypoint engraving – most of his work sells through art galleries in the United States and Canada. Another living descendant of Renoir is Alain, the son of Jean Renoir, who became a successful film producer. He is head of the Department of English Literature at the University of California at Berkeley. There is also of course, myself.

I am very happy to see the Renoir Museum and Garden open to visitors, and delighted that Derek Fell with the help of Michel Colas decided to produce a book that features the unusual garden. It is one of those very special places that never fails to lift your spirits no matter what time of year. Not only is it easy to see why Renoir wanted to save the place from destruction and live there, but if you look around at the old farmhouse and thread your way along the garden paths among the trees, or walk into his large studio that is virtually the same as when he left it, you can almost feel the presence of Renoir, his wife Aline, his model Gabrielle, Baptistin (a gardener and chauffeur) and all the other people who helped make Les Collettes one of the happiest and most inspirational households in France.

Dawn over the Mediterranean at Cagnes, seen from the hilltop at Les Collettes. Although today views of the sea from the house and garden are largely obscured by tall trees, in Renoir's day the family could sit on the terrace and watch the fishermen return to shore with boatloads of sardines.

DIRECT DESCENDANTS OF RENOIR

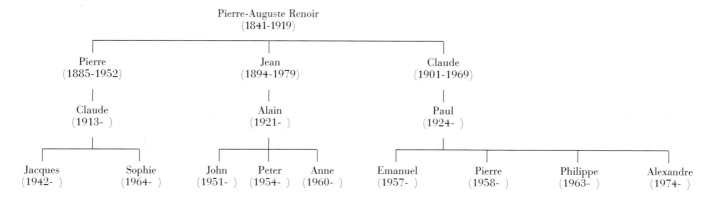

Pierre-Auguste Renoir
(1841-1919)

Pierre (1885-1952) — Jean (1894-1979) — Claude (1901-1969)

Claude (1913-) / Alain (1921-) / Paul (1924-)

Jacques (1942-), Sophie (1964-) / John (1951-), Peter (1954-), Anne (1960-) / Emanuel (1957-), Pierre (1958-), Philippe (1963-), Alexandre (1974-)

CHAPTER I

LES COLLETTES
A VISION OF EARTHLY
PARADISE

'The story of Cagnes and Renoir is a love story . . .
Cagnes seemed to be waiting for Renoir, and he
adopted it.' *Jean Renoir*

Renoir bought Les Collettes in 1907 and took possession of his Eden. The painter had not planned to buy property in the south: he already had a comfortable farmhouse in Burgundy, his wife's homeland, and for his regular winter sojourns he rented an apartment in Cagnes. The news that an ancient olive orchard overlooking the village was threatened by a development scheme made Renoir change his mind, and on an impulse he bought the site for himself. He intended to keep Les Collettes as it was, preserving its unique wildness and simplicity. Through his wife's encouragement, he found himself living there in a newly built house while the inspiring landscape was brought to life by the lively entourage of his family, his models, servants and visiting friends, and was immortalized in the paintings he produced in his fruitful last years. He also succeeded in conserving the atmosphere that so attracted him to the place.

Renoir had first come to the South of France as a bachelor with Claude Monet in the 1880s in search of new subjects to paint and to visit the artist Paul Cézanne. Together he and Monet encountered the strong colours and extraordinary light of the Mediterranean coast and both were enthusiastic about what they saw: 'What lovely landscapes, with distant horizons, and the most beautiful colours . . .', wrote Renoir. Overjoyed by the clarity of the light, the rugged grandeur of the coast and the exotic plants, they debated how to capture the scenes and colours on canvas, challenging each other to evoke the best impressions of what they saw.

By 1904 a further attraction was drawing Renoir to the south: the mild winter climate of the Midi. At this time the French Riviera – Cannes and Nice in particular – was exclusively a winter resort: summer holidays in the sun had not yet become fashionable. It was the region's mild winters that attracted the visitors, many of them fleeing the northern cold for the sake of their health, as Renoir himself decided to do. He was now sixty-three and, with Monet, was regarded as one of the greatest painters of his age. However, his health had deteriorated ever since a cycling accident in 1897 in which he had fallen on gravel and broken his arm. The accident brought on a severe attack of rheumatism and thereafter his hands became progressively more twisted and he found increased difficulty in walking. In 1888 he had experienced some paralysis of the facial muscles which gave his already gaunt face a fixed expression and an

Previous pages:
Left An ancient olive tree stands sentinel in the grounds of Les Collettes. This vista extends past clumps of wild oat grasses to the medieval village of Cagnes.
Right The front gable of the main house is framed by a rich assortment of trees and shrubs. The large arched window belongs to Renoir's former studio. This view is from the top of a flight of steps leading to a cobblestone courtyard in front of the old farmhouse.

Right A view of the lower village of Cagnes, with the foothills of the Maritime Alps in the distance, is shown in Renoir's atmospheric 1905 study, *Cros-de-Cagnes.*

In the lower garden at Les Collettes, leaves and trees frame a view of the hilltop village of Haut-de-Cagnes. Renoir's friend Georges Rivière wrote: 'There was one place he was particularly fond of. Sitting under a big lime [linden] tree, he would see on the opposite hill the village of Cagnes, with its old houses climbing the slope, huddled against one another and with clumps of orange trees showing amongst them. . . The slopes of Les Collettes, and the wide valley which separates the two hills, are covered with a variety of perfumed trees; and a mass of undergrowth of every shade carpets the earth.'

emaciated appearance. From 1902 onwards – following severe attacks of rheumatism and a partial atrophy of a nerve in the left eye which worsened his facial expression – his health deteriorated significantly. The family – his wife Aline, their three young sons and various other members of the household – developed a pattern of spending their summers partly in Paris and partly in Burgundy, and then moving south for the winter months. Each October the entourage would take the train from Paris to the Côte d'Azur.

They lodged in the lower part of Haut-de-Cagnes village. 'The story of Cagnes and Renoir is a love story', Jean Renoir later wrote of his father. Renoir often told Jean that he knew nothing in the world more beautiful than the valley of the little Cagne river at that particular moment when the dramatic outline of the Baou mountain at Saint-Jeannet could just be made out through the reeds which gave the river its name. Fed by melting snows from the mountains, the river winds its way through a steep gorge just before the village, then transforms into marshland before entering the Mediterranean. 'Cagnes seemed to be waiting for Renoir,' Jean wrote, 'and he adopted it.' He liked to explore the roads around the little smallholdings, and several times he had been across the valley to Les Collettes, an old farm set in the midst of terraced vineyards, olive groves and orange orchards.

The name Les Collettes means a region of small hills, like those that cluster around Cagnes, near Nice, in the area between the southern face of the Maritime Alps and the Mediterranean. The steep slope with its 148 olive trees formed a crescent-shaped orchard around a terraced meadow. Half-hidden among the olives was the old farmhouse with weathered green shutters and a roof of terracotta tiles, its walls festooned with rambling vines. For forty years the farmstead had afforded a modest livelihood to an Italian peasant household, Madame Catherine Canova and her bachelor son Paul, who farmed the land with the aid of a donkey named Litchou.

Les Collettes looks across a little valley to the medieval village of Haut-de-Cagnes clinging to a steep hillside. Its tiny narrow streets and flights of steps rise up to an ancient fortified castle once owned by the Grimaldi family, from whom Prince Rainier of Monaco is descended. At the turn of the century this housed the local fire brigade, and the steep cobbled streets below clattered with the sound of donkeys' hoofs. Life in Cagnes was prosperous and slow. Lower down the hill the villagers made a good living from sardine fishing and market gardening. With its

mild, almost frost-free climate the region was renowned for its cultivation of flowers, particularly roses and carnations. Tender plants flourished here, and flamboyant bougainvillea covered walls and terraces. Fields full of lavender flowered in early summer and were harvested for the scent factories at Grasse, twenty miles away. The hillsides around were spangled with silvery olive trees, green clumps of oak and lime (linden) and dark umbrella pines, and everywhere was a profusion of wild culinary herbs – savory, thyme and rosemary, chicory with its bright blue flowers, camomile, oregano and fennel. On the roadsides pink mallow, purple oxalis and red poppies seeded themselves freely. Hidden in the

The landscape around Cagnes was an endless source of inspiration to Renoir. *View of Cagnes* (*c.* 1900) is one of the many serene and richly hued canvases that he produced in the last years of his life.

The ancient olive trees, gnarled and contorted with age, are features of the sun-scorched landscape of the Mediterranean.

long grass were chirping cicadas – the ever-present sound of the Midi.

One day in Cagnes Renoir received a visit from a villager who wanted him to know that the widow who owned Les Collettes had been approached to sell the land. A nurseryman wanted the property not for its olive trees, which would be removed, but to raise carnations for the florist trade. Renoir could not bear to think of the venerable olives being uprooted, the tenants of the old farmhouse evicted and the site transformed into a nursery. He summoned his driver Baptistin and in a horse and carriage drove up the hill to the property. As he stood among the grand old olive trees and gazed out at the shimmering Mediterranean to the south, and the village of Haut-de-Cagnes outlined against the distant mountains directly ahead, Renoir realized he *had* to buy the land.

Explaining his father's passion for the old olive trees, Jean Renoir later wrote that Renoir said they were the most beautiful trees he had ever seen. They were vast, gnarled, fossil-like and had stood for centuries, surviving savage storms, merciless droughts, unskilled pruning and long periods of total neglect – all these hardships conspiring to mould them into unusual shapes, giving them near-human characteristics. Renoir returned home, resolved to buy the property. The thought of seeing such noble trees turned into 'napkin rings, paperweights and wooden spoons' was unbearable. Madame Renoir visited the owner and an agreement of sale was made.

Renoir was content to see the property saved from destruction, and would not think of moving into the old farmhouse, which he preferred to keep the way it was – seemingly as old as the landscape itself. However, Madame Renoir could not bear the thought of owning land without building a home on it. She felt that here Renoir could have a house befitting his status, where he could entertain and work in peace. Renoir capitulated. He agreed that Aline should liaise with a professional architect from Nice on the design and construction of her dream house in a clearing on the highest part of the slope within sight of the old farmhouse, and that she could lay out a garden just below it. In this way he was able to preserve all the elements that contributed to the old-world atmosphere of the place, and at the same time satisfy Aline's strong nesting instinct.

Renoir had married Aline Charigot, a favourite model, relatively late in life,

In springtime at Les Collettes the terraces are bright with drifts of Mediterranean wild flowers including red poppies, blue anchusa and yellow euphorbia.

Firmly rooted along the grassy terrace – and seemingly cast in stone – a grand old pair of olive trees thrust their strong branches of silvery leaves skyward. A white-flowering cherry tree (left) enlivens the background with an avalanche of blossoms. Young, shrub-like citrus trees line the lower terrace. The Mediterranean Sea and Cap d'Antibes are just visible in the background.

Renoir's passion for old trees is evident in *Landscape on the Coast, near Menton*, painted in the vicinity of Cagnes in 1883 when he and Claude Monet travelled together along the Mediterranean coast between Marseilles and Genoa. These majestic olive trees cling to the rugged cliff-top, their shadowy forms contrasting with the bright sun-drenched coastal headlands and the sapphire-blue sea.

Gabrielle was Renoir's favourite model. A cousin of Aline, she joined the household as a maid and later left to marry the painter Conrad Slade.

Claude Renoir was born when his father was almost 60 years old. An attractive boy, he was often the subject of Renoir's paintings. He inherited Les Collettes when he was 18 and made a name for himself as a ceramist.

when he was almost fifty. Aline, eighteen years his junior, gave birth to their first son five years before their marriage. His experiences in early life moulded Renoir into a pragmatic, frugal man uninterested in a show of material wealth, and apprehensive of being tied down. His own father was a tailor of modest income, and in 1844, when Renoir was three, the family had moved from Limoges to Paris. To help the family finances, Renoir left school at thirteen and took a job painting miniatures on cups and plates in a porcelain factory. This career was cut short within a few years – when the innovation of a mass-production technique using transfers made hand-decorating obsolete – and Renoir became unemployed. By now, however, he had decided to try to pursue a career as a serious painter. At the age of twenty he enrolled at the studio of Charles Gleyre and, since a proper art education also required attendance at the Ecole des Beaux-Arts and acceptance at the annual Salon exhibitions, he simultaneously began a course of studies there.

The 1870 Franco-Prussian war and the Paris Commune hostilities that followed made the already precarious existence of a struggling artist even harder. These influences, together with his artistic ambitions, fostered a keen independence of spirit in Renoir. For many years he led the life of a bachelor and remained reluctant to put down roots, preferring to rent places to live, mostly around Paris. He travelled widely in Europe, visiting museums and galleries, eager to explore and analyse the work of the great masters before him.

As he grew older, however, Renoir had begun to consider the advantages of a stable married life – especially the companionship and comfort it would bring in his advancing years and the security it would provide for his children. By the time they came to Cagnes the Renoirs had three children: Pierre, almost in his twenties, Jean, aged ten, and Claude (nicknamed Coco), just three years old. The household also included Aline's young cousin Gabrielle Renard, who had come as a nursemaid when Jean was a baby, and who often modelled for Renoir, in addition to a varying cast of servants and other models who were always in attendance. Renoir's exhibitions had already brought him fame and fortune. After years of poverty, when he had often had to forgo a meal to buy artist's materials, he was no longer poor.

The new main house at Les Collettes was completed in the autumn of 1908. It was quite grand and had running water, electricity, central heating provided by a

Above A detail from *Portrait of Madame Renoir with Bob* (*c.* 1910), one of several canvases Renoir painted of his wife, Aline.

Left A Canary Island date palm towers above the main residence and punctuates the cloudless summer sky with its graceful cluster of shimmering green fronds. Below, a group of yuccas display tapering flower spikes of waxy white florets.

big boiler, and a telephone (the house interior is described in Chapter 5). Renoir disliked the austere architecture and never included the new house in his paintings. The building is indeed strikingly plain, but when one realizes that Madame Renoir's intention was to see it curtained with wisteria and large-leaved ivy, which either died off or never took a hold, it does not seem so out of character. Nor was Renoir particularly satisfied with the stark interior, but he did like the balconies. These offered spectacular views of the mountains and the sea, with the rocky pine-clad Cap d'Antibes silhouetted at the end of a vast silvery arc of beach where fishermen pulled up their boats and dried their nets.

A large formal garden below the house was planted out in the spring of 1908, and a kitchen garden with an extensive artichoke patch was established at the other end of the property, behind the farmhouse. There were also the orchards and vineyards, plus glasshouses for growing carnations and vegetables all year round. In an enthusiastic letter to a family friend Renoir compared himself to the octogenarian in a French fable: 'We are in the process of planting, like La Fontaine's old man . . . The green peas are doing well, and so are the potatoes. So for the moment it's perfect bliss.'

Renoir expressed little interest in the formal garden and left the design and planting of it to Aline. Although he did not depict its layout in any of his paintings, he later drew up plans to transform it into a Florentine garden, and actually placed his sculpture of *Venus Victrix* there as its focal point. The flowers that Aline grew were another matter, and provided an endless source of inspiration. Renoir frequently painted roses grown in the formal garden, as well

A view of the pine grove from Renoir's bedroom window. The silvery leaves of olive trees (right) contrast with the cloud-like leaf canopy of umbrella pines (centre).

as the wonderful arrangements of freshly cut flowers from the numerous flower beds which Aline established in different parts of the property.

Once Renoir's family and retinue were settled in at Les Collettes, the planning and planting of the garden progressed quickly. Wide paths were constructed to make most parts of the site easily accessible by wheelchair, to which Renoir was to be more or less confined after 1912. Many different kinds of shade tree already grew on the property, and others were planted in strategic locations. Shade was especially important since Renoir had sensitive skin that could burn easily in the Mediterranean sun. A grove of tall umbrella pines offered pleasant shade in the lower garden, and there were several handsome Canary Island date palms. Close to the house a fast-growing eucalyptus with weeping branches of silvery-blue fragrant leaves and aromatic bark was planted – an Australian native that acclimatizes well and looks at home in the Midi.

Below Near the highest point at Les Collettes, a Canary Island date palm rises from a bed of deep blue bearded iris in spring. The palm's decorative orange flower clusters erupt from its crown. The blue of the iris flowers and the plant's soft blue-green leaves echo the colours of the nearby sea.

Left A broad flight of steps with narrow risers gently descends a slope from the top of the garden to a cobblestone courtyard. Red and pink ivy-leaf pelargoniums spill over a retaining stone wall (right) while a tangle of flowering shrubs (left) scrambles up metal supports.

But much of the inherent wildness of Les Collettes remained. The essence of the estate — the old-world farmhouse in its olive grove — was valiantly preserved by Renoir, who saw in it 'an idealized vision of past society', in the words of the art historian John House. 'Renoir's view of nature necessarily implied the human presence, which the olives and the old farm evoked so richly; often . . . figures beside the house and beneath the trees enliven the scene still further. The harmonious interrelationship between nature and the traces of man became the vision of the "earthly paradise" which he sought in his art in his last years. As Grappe put it in 1933, "The farm at Les Collettes is the decor of his flamboyant fantasy."''

The Garden of Eden had its serpent, and Renoir's Eden featured its own mischief-making element. For his two younger sons Les Collettes was a marvellous playground in which they could climb trees, keep pets and generally run wild. One morning Renoir looked out of his bedroom window to find that an orderly line of sweet orange trees laden with fruit had been stripped bare; in robbing the trees of their fruit, the boys had also inflicted terrible damage to the branches. His reaction was to have these sweet orange trees replaced with varieties bearing only sour, inedible fruit, thus removing temptation and assuring him of his view of beautiful orange-studded trees.

Left In summer the flower borders at Les Collettes are enlivened by a confusion of ivy-leaf pelargoniums which spill over retaining walls.

Below A strawberry tree stands outside the entrance of the main house at Les Collettes, one of several fine specimens that Renoir admired. Decorative, small, urn-shaped flowers are followed by edible orange and red strawberry-like fruit clusters that ripen in the autumn.

hutches as well as the donkey, and always people coming and going taking care of daily chores.

A magnificent ancient olive tree with wild flowers sprouting between its roots stands sentinel at the top of a broad flight of steps which descends to a cobblestone courtyard beside the farmhouse. In summer the drystone retaining wall edging the steps is bright with cascades of brilliant red and pink ivy-leaf pelargoniums; and in spring it is crowned with a massive undulating bed of blue bearded iris. The cobblestone yard is encircled by large shady deciduous trees, including a strawberry tree (*Arbutus unedo*) and a lime or linden (*Tilia platyphyllos*).

Above and below The patina of the roof tiles (above), the faded shutters and the muted tones of the weathered plaster walls (below) contribute to the rustic charm of the old farmhouse.

Left Pink-flowering angel's trumpet blooms prolifically during spring and summer.

Far left The farmhouse, drenched in sunlight, seen through olive branches.

The two-storey farmhouse is typical of many in the fertile valleys of the Midi, and Renoir painted it many times. In its setting of wild orchard and unmown grass it seems to embody so many elements Renoir valued in his garden: textural qualities rather than bright colour – the patina of old iron, the dull shine of a roof tile, fading olive-green paint on a shutter, pitted plaster, the gnarled, wrinkled bark of an encroaching olive tree. A wooden balcony with an ornate iron railing and metal frame canopy supports an array of flowering vines and flowers in hanging baskets; the expanse of plastered walls is softened by a rich assortment of shrubs including a blue-flowering tree tomato (*Cyphomandra crassicaulis*, syn. *C. betacea*), which bears edible scarlet fruits like small plums in spring, and several kinds of angel's trumpets (*Brugmansia* species). Angel's trumpets – also known as daturas – have large, translucent lance-like leaves and magnificent pendulous trumpet-shaped blossoms in pink, white and yellow. At times their heady fragrance seems intoxicating, and in fact the whole plant is poisonous. At Les Collettes these tropical South American shrubs lose their leaves in winter, but still reach tree-like heights. They are planted around the main house as well as by the farmhouse.

There is an old carriage shed with large double doors; adjoining the farmhouse is an outdoor bakery, with its brick oven for baking bread and pizza and, nearby, an old washhouse with a large metal trough for washing clothes. Washerwomen became a favourite theme in Renoir's paintings at Les Collettes, though *Washerwomen at Cagnes* (*c.*1912) was painted near the little Cagne river, which ran close to the bottom of the property. Unlike his fellow Impressionist Monet, Renoir preferred landscapes with people in them, and in this last period of his life he was preoccupied more than ever in painting bathers, nymphs and nudes who seem to merge with the trees, fruits and flowers around them in a sumptuous celebration of nature.

Monet and Renoir were life-long friends, although their theories about painting had diverged in the early 1880s. They had first met in their twenties at the Académie Gleyre in Paris. Charles Gleyre's teaching was independent of the Ecole des Beaux-Arts and attracted many talented students, several of whom – including Alfred Sisley, Frédéric Bazille and, of course, Renoir himself – were to emerge as famous Impressionist painters. Students who failed entry into the Ecole could enrol with Gleyre and still receive sound artistic training. Although Renoir was accepted by the Ecole, he soon had a disagreement with his professor and left to rely instead on Gleyre's teaching methods which encouraged freedom of expression and experimentation. And so Renoir had met Monet, a fellow student just four months older than himself. They shared common interests besides a passion for artistic expression.

Renoir and Monet had been prime movers in a new approach to painting; for years previously painters had been content to compose realistic landscapes in their studios. (The English painter Thomas Gainsborough, for example, had painted some of his most lyrical landscapes by candlelight using cabbage stalks and sand as props for trees and land.) But helped by the recent invention of oil

Renoir and Claude Monet were life-long friends having first met in Paris during their student days. They lived and often travelled together, sometimes painting the same subjects. This affectionate portrait, *Claude Monet* (1872), is one of numerous studies Renoir made of Monet alone or with his family.

Above A rear view of the farmhouse showing the oven which was used for baking bread and pizza.

Left White-flowering angel's trumpet, a native of South America, is one of the many exotic species of the ornamental solanaceous plant family that grow around the foundations of both the old farmhouse and the main house.

paints in tubes, which were ready for immediate use and easy to carry, the Impressionists went out into the open air to paint. They were startled by the changes in colour as light varies, and had to abandon old notions of local colour tones which had held good in a studio where light came from only one direction. They translated everything they saw into sensations of colour and used small juxtaposed brushstrokes of paint straight from the tube so as to capture the immediacy of what their eyes beheld.

The laundry (left) and the main house at Les Collettes enjoyed the facility of piped water, but the new invention was a luxury that few other families in the Cagnes area could afford.

The sight of women washing laundry in a freshwater stream was soon to disappear with the advent of modern plumbing. In *Washerwomen at Cagnes* (*c.* 1912, above) the work is done under the comforting shade of a tall olive tree. Renoir conveys a sense of energy among the women as they wash, scrub, soak and wring out the washing; he also heightens the sense of activity by emphasizing the sinuous – almost writhing – trunk and branches of the tree, as if in imitation of the women's labour.

Renoir often expressed the view that theorizing about art was a time-wasting activity: 'I don't give a damn', he would say when asked his opinion. 'There is something in painting which cannot be explained, and that something is the essential. You come to Nature with your theories and she knocks them all flat.' He admired craftsmanship in a painting above everything else. Over the years, however, he became disillusioned with the constraints of Impressionism and in the 1880s broke away from it. 'It was a blind alley for me . . . a kind of painting that made you constantly compromise yourself.' If the unchanging light in a studio was a limitation, the fluctuation of natural light outdoors presented problems of a different kind. 'Light plays too great a part out of doors; you have no time to work out the composition – you can't see what you are doing.' For the remainder of the 1880s Renoir went through his 'Harsh' period – reverting to a more classical, realistic form of painting. But then came the last and – to some – the most glorious phase of his work, known as his 'Iridescent' period. From the Impressionists he retained his awareness of light, colour and warmth of tone, and from the classical period a superb sense of composition. Some of his best and most stimulating work was produced in these later years.

A clump of wild red poppies gleam out from the arid, stony soil.

Renoir still made use of the landscape around him, such as the bright, sunny, open meadow below the farmhouse. Across the top of it, a broad gravel path gently descends at an angle, and the senses are stunned by the sight of three enormous olive trees that appear to be petrified, they are so old. Beyond the trees is a clear view of the picturesque village of Haut-de-Cagnes, topped by its beautiful castle. The contrast between the natural tormented shapes of the trees and the man-made architectural beauty on the opposite hill is spellbinding.

When Renoir bought Les Collettes, it was covered with clumps of wild oat grasses with long seed-heads which would shimmer translucent silver and gold when backlit by the sun. He hated to see them cut. When the mistral blew across his meadow of wild grasses, it would create waves with a silvery sheen in spring, golden in autumn. The grass changed to emerald green in winter, and became jewelled in spring with the prettiest wild flowers imaginable. Tufts of lavender scented it in summer. Jean Renoir later wrote 'If I were taken blindfold to Les Collettes I am sure I would recognize it at once, just from the scent.' He thought the garden's fragrance infinitely more subtle and more memorable than the celebrated perfumes of the wild herbs of the maquis that cover the arid lands around Aix-en-Provence. He described how these grasses made him feel particularly close to his father.

As the sun crossed the sky there would be an ever-changing display of colour, depending on the season and the weather. Renoir, with his 'Impressionist eye', would study the changes as intently as watching a performance at the opera. On a misty morning at Les Collettes the colours of the landscape are muted, cool and almost monochromatic. As the mist dissipates with the strengthening sun, the orchard becomes saturated in sunlight, intensifying the colours. By late afternoon the colours change again as the setting sun infuses the daylight with strong reddish tones. After rainfall comes another world of colour contrasts, the grey trunks of the olive trees shining like coal.

Olive trees in other parts of the Mediterranean are small because heavy pruning has kept their branches close to the ground for easy harvesting. At Les Collettes, however, they have been allowed to grow unchecked, lifting a lofty canopy of

Yellow bird's-foot trefoil and red poppies bloom among the roots of the olive trees in spring.

Wild oat grasses commandeer a slope at Les Collettes in autumn. The golden seed-heads create fountain-like sprays of slender stems; the leaves rustle in the slightest breeze and glow when backlit by the sun. Renoir admired the natural beauty of the unmown grasses.

leafy branches high into the sky. They are not only large in girth, with hollowed trunks and deeply scored bark, but their branches of silvery slender leaves first stab the sky, then arch out and drape down in a weeping effect. It is believed that this olive grove was the inspiration of François I, who had his troops plant trees to keep them occupied during a truce in the wars against Emperor Charles V in the early sixteenth century. A local historian estimates that a few of the trees may be even older than that – perhaps nearly a thousand years old.

Unlike the oaks in a grove beyond the farmhouse, the olive trees at Les Collettes – despite their size – do not cast a dense shade that suffocates other

The rising sun steals into the garden at Les Collettes behind an olive tree, soon to cast long shadows across the grassy terraces and flood the meadow with sunlight. The sun rises from behind the Mediterranean Sea and has begun its magical play of light that so captivated the Impressionist painters.

growth; their shade is light and airy, allowing even grass to grow right up to the roots and wild flowers to germinate in hollows and cracks along the fissured bark. The roots of each tree extend long distances from the trunk, which is often flared at the base, giving the trees a good hold on the hilly terrain. Even in the strongest wind, the trunk stays as stiff and solid as a rock, the upper branches bending like a willow, and if the leaves themselves are shredded in a gale, in the calm aftermath the branches quickly leaf out anew. In the morning as the sun rises out of the sea and again in late afternoon as it dips behind the heights of Cagnes, the old trees pencil long shadows across the grassy clearings.

A cavity in the root of an olive tree provides nourishment and shelter for a sweet alyssum seedling.

Resembling the flow of solidified lava, roots of an ancient olive tree spread out to grasp a firm hold on the earth. The roots create a flared trunk that enables the tree to withstand high winds in exposed locations. After rainfall, as here, the olive trees take on subtle steel-grey tones.

The Garden at Les Collettes (1909) captures the wildness of the trees that Renoir so loved and is a fine example of his richly coloured, impressionistic celebration of the natural world.

Although Renoir admired the olive trees, he also regarded them with a degree of frustration: 'The olive tree! What a brute! If you realized how much trouble it has caused me! A tree full of colours. Not great at all. How all those little leaves make me sweat! A gust of wind and my tree's tonality changes. The colour isn't on the leaves, but in the spaces between them.' On another occasion he said, 'Look at the light on the olive trees . . . it shines like a diamond . . . it's pink, it's blue . . . and the sky that plays across them . . . it drives you mad!' Jean Renoir observed: 'The shadow cast by the olive trees was often mauve. It is in constant motion, luminous, full of gaiety and life.'

In Renoir's 1909 painting *The Garden at Les Collettes*, the landscape is bathed in golden sunlight, with the farmhouse in the background half-hidden by twisted trunks of olive trees. The shadows on these trees are deep purple, a substitute for

A tunnel-like vista, largely unchanged since Renoir's time, is formed by the strong, arching olive branches that frame the old stone farmhouse.

black, which was considered an almost sacrilegious colour for an artist to use at the time. But Renoir had used black boldly in his massive *Portrait of Madame Charpentier and her Children* which was accepted by the Salon in 1879. In this family picture the black-and-white dress of Madame Charpentier – the Rubenesque wife of a well-known publisher – echoes the black-and-white coat of the large Newfoundland dog at her feet; both contrast daringly with the ice-blue children's dresses and the flowery sumptuous, dining room. The critics and the public loved it. Camille Pissarro wrote of the occasion: 'Renoir is a great success at the Salon. I think he is launched. All the better! It's a hard life being poor.' At the age of thirty-eight the artist's future was secure, his portrait commissions now earning him a good living while allowing him to experiment freely with more satisfying subjects such as landscapes and the female nude.

The Bathers (*c.* 1901/2). This painting, on display at Les Collettes, is a re-working of an earlier study begun in the 1880s. It echoes the thematic and stylistic elements present in a larger, more finely finished canvas of the same title which today hangs in the Philadelphia Museum of Art in the United States of America.

Now Renoir's palette had lightened again: he no longer used pure black, but would mix red and cobalt or ultramarine for his shadows. Albert André, a great friend and fellow painter, who visited Renoir frequently at Les Collettes, has left a detailed account of how Renoir went about his painting during this period. First he would brush in a few sketchy guidelines, usually in reddish brown, so as to proportion the elements that would make up the picture – the 'volumes' as Renoir called them. Then he would dilute pure colours with a lot of turpentine, and spread them rapidly over the canvas, until you could see indefinite iridescent shapes appearing with all the tints running into one another. At the next session, when this first coat had dried, he would go to work on a second coat, this time using more colour mixed with turpentine and linseed oil. He would then apply highlights in pure white, and deepen the shadows and half-tints. Almost no mixing was done on the palette itself, which was covered with 'thin, oily, almost comma-like blobs of pure colour'. Little by little he would get his forms into shape, but always allowing them to mingle. '"I want them to kiss," he would say . . . A few more brushstrokes, and rising from the colour haze you saw the first soft forms, glistening like precious stones and wrapped in golden, translucent shadows.' The art critic Denis Rouart summarized this process: 'With his brush, Renoir would apply colour in thin, transparent layers, one over the other, each veiling the last without concealing it, so that he obtained a smooth, silky lustrous texture, full of deep limpid gleams.'

Renoir's outdoor studio at Les Collettes.

The olive grove was for Renoir a wild garden, an idyllic setting for his paintings. He had a wooden studio built among the trees with a corrugated iron roof like a garden shed. It had large windows on two sides hung with cotton curtains to regulate the light. The shed itself has long since disappeared, but the plan on page 101 shows where it stood. Crippled with rheumatism, Renoir would be carried to this outside studio each morning in his sedan chair – a wicker chair attached to two bamboo poles – or wheeled down, and all day he would paint. 'I don't think a day has passed without my painting', he once said. His work would always put him in a good mood.

At Les Collettes Renoir painted landscapes, still lifes, flowers, portraits – but above all he gloried in the nude and semi-nude female figure. While he worked in his shed, his model would be posed on the flower-strewn grass outside, the light filtering down through the silvery olive branches. His son Jean remembered him humming a little tune, letting out small gasps of pleasure. 'It's intoxicating', he would say. 'It's divine.' Many of his pictures of nudes of this period have olive trees, luxuriant grass and wild flowers as a background into which his voluptuous figures merge, so that the natural world appears as significant as the main figures. The art critic William Gaunt wrote of this time: 'In this landscape with its blue and purple mountains in the distance, its grey olives, its slight vibration in the air that told of the nearness of the land-locked sea, its pervading warmth of colour, the nude figure could be placed in its proper context, in its own country.'

Renoir adored painting the female figure. A woman should be painted 'like a

Renoir, shrouded in a warm blanket to protect him from chills, is carried in a chair slung with poles up a slope at Les Collettes. The bearers are Albert André, a painter and friend, and one of his resident models known as La Boulangère.

This small unfinished study of a peasant woman drawing water from a stone well, *Young Woman at the Well* (n.d.), is on display in the main house with other original oil paintings, sketches, sculpture and memorabilia.

beautiful fruit', he explained to his friend Ambroise Vollard, the picture dealer. 'If there hadn't been breasts, I don't think I would ever have painted figures.' All his life Renoir had shunned professional models. He preferred to choose girls from a working background and at Les Collettes looked forward to the olive harvest in winter when girls from the village would come with long poles to knock the ripe black olives from the trees on to blankets spread out beneath. He would always be on the alert for a model, preferably someone with a luminous peachy skin that 'took the light'. Some women who refused Renoir's request to pose later expressed regret as the genius of his art became more widely accepted and recognized.

In his later years Renoir tended to advise artists not to get romantically involved with their models, but his own wife Aline had been working in a grocer's when he first saw her and asked her to pose for him. Since she had become stout, her cousin Gabrielle, Jean's nursemaid, had taken her place as Renoir's favourite model. Gabrielle had a swarthy complexion and liked to walk around in bare feet dressed like a gypsy in colourful Romany clothes and flamboyant jewellery, with a rose over her ear. She had an easy-going personality and a sense of fun that Renoir loved, for he had a good sense of humour himself. Indeed sometimes it was difficult to tell when Renoir was being serious and when he was joking. While he was painting Gabrielle out of doors one day at Les Collettes, she picked up a ripe olive and was about to put it in her mouth when he cautioned her: 'Gabrielle, be careful, I don't think that's an olive — I think it's a goat dropping'. Gabrielle hesitated a second, put it in her mouth, and then spat it out. 'It *is* a goat dropping!' she exclaimed.

Renoir had begged Aline's permission to have Gabrielle pose in the nude, as it was still regarded as a little scandalous. For some years Gabrielle was part of the household, almost a second mother to Renoir's children and a frequent subject for his paintings. She eventually left to marry Conrad Slade, a painter from California, and lived with him in Beverly Hills until her death in 1959. Slade had fallen in love with her from seeing her portraits by Renoir.

Above Gabrielle in gypsy costume in *Dancing Girl with Castanets* (1909). Renoir's model was never as plump as she is depicted here, but he felt it was perfectly acceptable to embellish the physical features of the women who posed for him.

Left Renoir painting at Cagnes. Although his hands were badly deformed, he could still hold a brush between his thumb and forefinger. He continued to paint despite encroaching paralysis and unrelieved pain.

CHAPTER

III

THE GARDENS AROUND THE HOUSE

'In this marvellous country it seems as if
misfortune cannot befall one; one is cosseted by the
atmosphere.'   *Pierre-Auguste Renoir*

Above Daisies, poppies and yellow mustard create patches of colour in the unmown grass.

Previous pages:
Left Bearded irises make a strong show of colour at Les Collettes in April. In the background, wild flowers are starting to bloom in the grass.
Right Lavender, native to the Mediterranean, flowers prolifically beneath an olive tree.

Right In *The Dahlias (Garden in the rue Cortot, Montmartre)* (1876), Renoir painted the kind of natural garden he admired, with dahlias flowering freely in an overgrown lawn. In later years, when at Les Collettes, he encouraged the same kind of simple, carefree planting.

By the time Renoir acquired Les Collettes he had known many gardens. He had observed his friend Monet cultivate several gardens with an exuberance of flowers in *clos normand* or cottage-garden style, such as the famous flower garden he created in the old apple and plum orchard facing his house at Giverny. Renoir had seen many formal gardens in the Italian Renaissance style – both during travels in Italy and at the extravagant houses of his wealthy patrons around Paris, particularly the Château du Wargemont, home of Paul Bérard, a Paris banker. He had seen the highly formalized gardens of the Moors in Algeria and in the palaces of Spain. In England he had admired both the great estate gardens with their topiary architecture and sweeping lawns and the more naturalistic English style of planting with flowering perennials spilling on to the pathways.

Two gardens in particular had made a lasting impression on Renoir and provided inspiration for many of his paintings long before he discovered the landscape of Les Collettes. Both were in Montmartre, where Renoir had lived. As a bachelor he had rented a room in an old folly in the rue Cortot, and he had especially liked its large overgrown garden, which is depicted in his early painting *The Dahlias (Garden in the rue Cortot, Montmartre)*. It 'looked like a beautiful neglected park', wrote Renoir's friend, Georges Rivière. 'Outside the hallway of the little house, you found yourself facing a huge lawn of unmown grass dotted with poppies, convolvulus and daisies. Beyond that a fine avenue of trees and beyond that again an orchard and vegetable garden, then a shrubbery . . .'

The second garden was at Château des Brouillards, where Renoir lived for several years after he was married. The gardens there had seen better days. They too were overgrown, in need of care. Renoir loved them for that reason. What they lacked in orderliness and floral colour they surpassed with an abundance of interest in form, tone and texture. Roses grew with wild abandon, their blossoms shining like gems against a sea of green, while mature stands of deciduous trees produced exquisite qualities of light and dappled shade. Was it this garden or Bérard's rose garden at Wargemont that Van Gogh had in mind in 1888, during a period of melancholy? He wrote from Arles: 'You will remember that we saw a magnificent garden of roses by Renoir. I was expecting to find subjects like that here, and indeed, it was that way while the orchards were in bloom. Now the appearance of things has changed and become much harsher . . . You will

Above Echium fastuosum –
a shrubby perennial from
the Canary Islands – grows
spectacular tapering flower
spikes studded with tubular
blue flowers. It blooms freely
throughout the
Mediterranean in early
summer.

Right A mass of bearded iris
sweeps around a curved
flower bed in front of the
farmhouse in spring. The
smooth blue-green leaves of
the iris contrast with the
delicate light green foliage of
an overhanging lime (linden)
tree.

Left A white-flowering
cherry tree creates a
highlight on the front lawn.
Cherry trees were planted
throughout the garden, their
spring blossom coinciding
with drifts of blue iris visible
in the background.

probably have to go to Nice to find Renoir's garden again.'

Twenty years later Van Gogh's vision became a reality for Renoir. In the gentle
climate of Cagnes, just a few miles west of Nice, roses grew everywhere and in the
mild winters the citrus trees retained their fruit as if waiting for the spring
blossom to join them. The formal garden which Madame Renoir laid out was to
have a pattern of oranges and roses as its principal theme. Renoir's own
preference was for simple flowers, massed together without any complex
interplanting. He liked the bold dash of colour created by beds packed with single
varieties of flower — spring-flowering bearded iris in one area, winter-flowering
ivy-leaf pelargoniums in another, and patches of summer-flowering lavender
everywhere. When the sculptor Auguste Rodin visited Les Collettes, Madame
Renoir explained: 'There are no rare flowers here, but marguerites next to the
mimosa. My husband likes common or garden flowers.'

Renoir was kept informed of which flowering plants were coming into bloom,
and (since by now he was severely crippled) he would ask to be carried by sedan
chair to that part of the garden — sometimes simply to admire the display and at
other times to paint it. Through treatment by various doctors, Renoir's condition
would vary; occasionally he would have some remission, but by 1912 he was
unable to walk. Madame Renoir wrote to his dealer, Durand-Ruel: 'My husband

Above Dutch iris contribute
to a garden full of contrasts
of colour, atmosphere and
mood.

51

Above Marguerites (1905) shows an informal bouquet of flowering annuals – including red zinnias, white daisies and pink poppies – all examples of the 'common' flowers Renoir liked.

Below The broad, serrated paddle-shaped leaves of variegated agave.

is beginning to move his arms, though his legs are still the same. He can't stand upright, though he's getting used to being immobile. It is heart-breaking to see him in this state.'

Sometimes Renoir would be wheeled down to Madame Renoir's formal rose garden just to admire the blooms. To reach this garden, you take the broad gravel path downhill from the farmhouse passing first an exotically planted dry slope where tender cacti and succulents thrive in the Mediterranean climate. There are variegated agaves (*Agave americana* 'Variegata'), natives of Mexico, forming gigantic rosettes of fleshy, arching spiky leaves, richly coloured in contrasting bands of yellow and blue-green. The mature plants produce long slender flower stalks topped with large clusters of yellow-green tubular flowers; once they have bloomed the plants die, but they seed freely as well as producing offsets. At Les Collettes they also colonize boundary walls in groups of twos and threes, between clumps of shrubs. Flowering stems of yucca species shoot skywards from this dry slope, at first resembling gigantic asparagus spears, then opening up into a candelabra of glistening white waxy flowers. Elsewhere in the sunny beds and borders are *Beschorneria yuccoides* (Mexican yucca), succulents with blue-green fleshy leaves which, in early spring, produce tall arching coral-red flower stems, topped with coral bracts and jade-green flowers.

As you approach the formal garden, looking back uphill, beyond the cacti, you see the main house with its Mediterranean-style terrace, ground-floor archways and prominent balconies dominating this part of the hillside. Renoir's glance would perhaps not have lingered on these architectural features so much as on the roses that curtained them. Roses grew everywhere here and were trained up the walls and around the archways below his bedroom window. On the retaining walls of the formal garden immediately below the main house they rambled high, producing an avalanche of mostly red and pink blooms. First to flower in spring was always the vigorous yellow-flowered Lady Banks's or Banksian rose (*Rosa banksiae* 'Lutea'), its arching stems smothered in clusters of small double blooms which then dropped their petals like confetti over the path.

Renoir had a fine collection of highly fragrant old-fashioned roses and also modern varieties, particularly the new race known as Hybrid Teas. These grew extra large flowers, one hefty bloom to a stem, and had the fragrance of Indian tea. The clear light of the Midi and the cool summer nights encouraged roses to

Left Beschorneria yuccoides, a spring-flowering succulent with handsome coral-red plumes and nodding green florets, arches over a pathway below the main house.

Above A ceramic plate with a plum motif designed by Renoir's youngest son Coco provides the background to a single rose on a shelf in the dining room.

grow fast and bloom spectacularly. At Cap d'Antibes, within sight of Les Collettes, Meilland – the leading French rose breeders – established a rose farm which is still there today, in spite of land values reaching astronomical heights. Meilland breed roses both for growing under glass for the cut-flower industry and for garden display, and it is estimated that one out of every three roses sold throughout the world originates from them. They bred the universally renowned 'Peace' at the outbreak of the Second World War, though it had to wait until peace was declared to be named and released to the gardening public.

Another local rose breeder, Henri Lambic, honoured Renoir with a new rose in

Right The delicate full-blown blooms of a wichuraiana rambler contrast with the bold green of its leaves and the stone wall behind.

Below A modern Hybrid Tea in a corner of the rose garden.

Left Still Life: Roses (n.d.). Renoir's floral compositions, explorations of texture and form, were often painted as preliminary studies for more complex works. Almost every day at Les Collettes he would paint a vignette of a cluster of flowers, fruits or vegetables gathered from the gardens.

1909, naming it 'Painter Renoir'. It promptly received an Award of Merit from the Horticultural Society of Nice. A shrub rose that proved to be both hardy and heat-tolerant, it has long arching thorny branches covered in pale pink semi-double flowers, up to 10 centimetres/4 inches across and slightly fragrant. This is the predominant rose in the formal garden at Les Collettes today, a number of them surviving from those originally planted by Aline.

Roses were Renoir's favourite flowers, and many of his paintings include them. Women wear roses in their hair, as corsages, or hold them in bouquets. Even in the portrait Renoir painted in 1917 of Ambroise Vollard – dressed as a toreador – a rose lies at his feet. Roses are a theme that runs throughout Renoir's career, and had a special significance in his artistic development.

Renoir's father had come from Limoges, famous for its delicate china, and it was in a porcelain factory in Paris which produced copies of Sèvres and Limoges designs for export to the Far East that Renoir had served his apprenticeship. In his early days there, he was confined to painting borders of plates and saucers, firstly with little sprigs of flowers at five sous a time, then with larger swags of roses. Later he was allowed to paint the central figures, usually daintily tinted shepherdesses and, later still, a portrait of Marie Antoinette featuring a peaches-and-cream complexion and low neckline. It was here that he might first have

Below Climbing roses mingle with the ripening fruits of a tree tomato.

Far right Gabrielle with a Rose (1911). Renoir's later paintings combine a classically inspired sense of composition with an impressionistic awareness of the nuances of colour, light, tone and texture. In this portrait, the flowers accentuate the soft rose-tinted tones of his subject, emphasizing her colour, complexion and voluptuousness.

noticed the way rose tints flatter a woman's complexion. When transfer designs took over from hand painting, Renoir decorated fans and window blinds. In his spare time he would visit the Louvre (the family lived nearby in a poor area of Paris next to the Tuileries Palace) and he became a life-long admirer of the painters Watteau, Boucher and Fragonard (who himself came from Grasse); they all used roses to enhance their paintings. Renoir assiduously copied aspects of their work to improve his skills as a porcelain painter.

From his apprenticeship at the porcelain factory Renoir had also discovered the subtlety that could be achieved through using a tapering round flexible brush rather than the flat-ended kind the Impressionists were to become so fond of.

Renoir not only included roses in his paintings to draw out the luminous quality of a model's skin, but also painted studies of roses as experiments in flesh tones. Whereas Monet liked roses because they helped carry colour high into the sky — climbing roses covered the metal archways spanning the Grande Allée at Giverny, creating a floral canopy and a dramatic element for Monet's pictorial composition — Renoir adored roses because he saw in them the colours of the children and women he loved to paint. 'When I'm painting flowers,' he declared, 'I can experiment boldly with tones and values without worrying about

Right In addition to the 1909 shrub rose named after the artist, 'Painter Renoir', shown here, the rose garden at Les Collettes features a large collection of old roses planted among orderly lines of citrus trees and along the house walls. These old roses have the heaviest perfume.

The rose garden in early spring with 'Painter Renoir' shrub roses in the foreground and orange-studded trees beyond.

destroying the whole painting. I could not dare to do that with a figure, because I would be afraid of spoiling everything. The experience I gain from these experiments can be applied to my paintings.' But he claimed it cost him little effort to create some of his most beautiful works. As he told his friend Walter Pach, 'I arrange my subject as I want it, then I go ahead and paint it, like a child. I want a red to be sonorous, to sound like a bell; if it doesn't turn out that way, I add more reds and other colours until I get it. I'm no cleverer than that. I have no rules and no methods . . . I look at a nude: there are myriads of tiny tints. I must find the ones that will make the flesh on my canvas live and quiver.'

Madame Renoir laid out the formal garden with four rows of citrus trees (mostly oranges and tangerines), seven to each row, interplanted with rose bushes. In spring the combination of bright orange fruit and pink rose blossoms is stunning – reminiscent of the old Roman fresco painted for Augustus Caesar's wife Livia at their summer villa outside Rome. This shows orange trees among which roses, poppies, irises and daisies grow with wild abandon – very much in the spirit of Les Collettes. It is possible that Renoir saw this fresco on his travels in Italy. Towards the top of the formal garden a bare brick pedestal marks the spot where Renoir originally placed his bronze sculpture, *Venus Victrix*. A contemporary photograph shows a rose, heavy with blossom, trailing over the pedestal.

It was Vollard who suggested to Renoir that he might try sculpture. Renoir had been impressed when the sculptor Aristide Maillol had come to make a bust of him, and it is Maillol's work that shows its influence in Renoir's. By now Renoir was severely crippled and did not have the strength in his fingers to make a clay model. Indeed, as his hands grew more painful and tender, he could only clasp a paintbrush with the aid of a cushion of lint in his hand, but his addictive desire to paint made him conquer his handicap. Now, for his sculpture, the help of a young Catalan sculptor, Richard Guino, was sought. Renoir would stand back and direct him with a stick. Vollard recalled, 'Many a time I would find him standing under the silvery olive trees in his garden, a long wand in his hand, directing the work of the sculptor. "You see, Vollard, it's as though my hand were at the end of the stick. To do good work I shouldn't be too near. How can I see what I am doing with the clay right under my nose?"'

Renoir completed about twenty-four important pieces of sculpture during these twilight years of his life. Those at Les Collettes include a beautiful head as well as a medallion of his small son Coco, a bust of Madame Renoir, a bearded shepherd, a little girl washing, a blacksmith and the *Venus Victrix*, of which six bronze casts were made between 1914 and 1916, one of which is at Les Collettes. Others are in the Petit Palais museum in Paris, the Tate Gallery, London, and the Baltimore Art Museum in the United States of America. Two are in private collections. One of these is the centrepiece at Brenthurst, the estate of Harry Oppenheimer in Johannesburg, South Africa. The Brenthurst garden is one of the most beautiful in the world, and Venus stands resplendent in a clearing on a lawn, surrounded by exotic trees. In his book *The Brenthurst Gardens* Alan H. Smith describes the effect of *Venus Victrix* here:

Above Bust of Coco, in the drawing room of the main house. Long hair for boys was popular among French families at the time.

'The main lawns below the house provide a broad and uncluttered setting for Renoir's figure of . . . *Venus Victrix*. The Roman goddess of love stands victorious after being judged to be the most beautiful of goddesses; she holds the Golden Apple of Discord, which prompted the contest when it was thrown down to be awarded to the fairest . . . The proportions and features of the figure are reminiscent of Renoir's paintings, in particular his series of bathers and his later nudes, but the demeanour of Venus suggests more of the serenity of a goddess than the lust for life he saw in French country women.'

Keith Wheldon in his book on Renoir has described *Venus Victrix* as having 'all the grace and amplitude of gesture found in Classical sculpture. The head is small, the neck firm and erect like a column, the shoulders describe soft and even curves rendered asymmetrical by the position of the arms, and the full serene volumes of the torso balance the figure in its gentle movement expressed in the positioning of the legs.'

Above This bust of Aline Renoir – moved from the garden into the main house – was originally displayed, almost hidden among shrubs, on a pedestal near the old farmhouse.

Never was a more beautiful statue intended for display in a garden. Renoir wanted to make it a permanent feature in the formal garden at Les Collettes and was planning to surround the statue on its pedestal with Grecian columns to create the effect of a ruined temple. It would have been a wonderfully romantic touch, but alas he died before he could carry out the scheme. The sculpture now stands on the broad terrace below the main house, for security reasons.

Her bronze skin shining from a light shower of rain, Renoir's most famous sculpture, *Venus Victrix*, is said to have captivated Picasso and influenced his art. The silvery blue tousled leaves of an olive tree behind her head complement the sculpture's majesty and metallic shine.

The path that makes a loop around the bottom of the formal garden is lined with oleander (*Nerium oleander*), a Mediterranean native. With its attractive narrow leaves this bushy evergreen shrub makes a good screening hedge or windbreak, and blooms profusely in summer, mostly with flowers in white and shades of pink, red and salmon. The flower clusters are attractive in arrangements – though the plant itself is very poisonous. Renoir had an avenue of oleanders lining the path leading down from the formal garden to the pine grove at the bottom of the property.

Renoir considered the umbrella pine (*Pinus pinea*) one of the most beautiful trees in the natural landscape, not only for its textured bark, which has reddish-brown patches deeply fissured with a tracery of black, but also for its lofty umbrella-like canopy. He painted groves of these trees at nearby Juan-les-Pins, Antibes and Menton. A fine mature specimen survives in the garden today, with younger pines creating a small grove.

Yellow Hybrid Tea roses and gazanias make colourful companions.

The path ascends on the east side of the formal garden towards the main house. A flight of curving steps garlanded with a massive Banksian rose leads up to a broad sunny terrace. Fragrant climbing roses and a vigorous shrub verbena, *Lantana camara*, decorate the arches that support the balcony below Renoir's bedroom window. This verbena is the type most commonly planted throughout the Mediterranean, its prickly stem producing round heads of little pink or yellow flowers which turn to orange or red and have a particularly sweet scent.

In the shelter of the arches are clustered potted plants – arum lilies, cinerarias in season, papyrus and spider plants. The arum or calla lilies (*Zantedeschia aethiopica*) do well here in the half-shade. Renoir loved their arrow-shaped twisting leaves, their strong erect flower stems and the elegant white flower spathe with its conspicuous powdery yellow spadix. Elsewhere in the garden clumps of these grow in shady, moist areas. The tender cinerarias (correctly *Pericallis* × *hybrida* but more popularly known as *Cineraria* or *Senecio* hybrids) are used extensively for bedding in early spring around the Mediterranean. They are also grown in cool greenhouses as pot plants, and in Renoir's garden are mostly planted in containers, which is how he painted them. Renoir especially liked the bicoloured ones, with white and red or white and blue combined in the same daisy-like flower.

Parallel to the house, close to the terrace balustrade, is a narrow rectangular

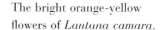

The bright orange-yellow flowers of *Lantana camara*.

Above The star-shaped flowers of oleander.

Previous pages:
Left Ivy-leaf pelargoniums overflow from an urn. Pink datura and vibrant red fuchsias are also in full bloom (right).
Right One of Renoir's favourite places to sit was under the cooling shade of the lime (linden) tree.

Below Blue *Agapanthus africanus*.

bed with a line of calamondin orange trees interplanted with *Agapanthus africanus* (African lily; blue lily of the Nile). The deep blue agapanthus flower umbels above their arching strap-like leaves present a good contrast to the golden-yellow fruits and dark, glossy oval foliage of the orange trees. The leaves of the agapanthus are attractive for most of the year, the slender flowering stems appearing in summer.

Following the gaze of Venus past mounds of white marguerite daisies (*Argyranthemum frutescens*) – whose abundance of flowers in spring completely hides their foliage – the terrace ends abruptly and becomes a broad rustic path beneath the shade of the towering eucalyptus and a stately Canary Island date palm (*Phoenix canariensis*). Perhaps no tree signals a mild climate more clearly than this palm with its strongly criss-cross-patterned trunk, graceful arching fronds and bright orange fruit clusters. Renoir loved to paint these beautiful trees, and there are two specimens elsewhere at Les Collettes.

Here too is a huge broad-leaved lime or linden tree (*Tilia platyphyllos*), spreading its cool shade over an informal patio area, where a pair of slatted benches face Haut-de-Cagnes. This was one of Renoir's favourite spots in the garden. After lunch the family and their visitors would sit out here in the shade, drinking coffee, talking and savouring the comforting sights, smells and sounds of the garden.

From between the shaded patio and the farmhouse courtyard a broad cobblestone path – actually a driveway – leads uphill in a graceful curve towards the front of the main house, which faces north. Along the house foundations is an assortment of flowering shrubs and vines – tree fuchsias loaded with flowers, pink angel's trumpets, pink-blossomed oleander and powder-blue vining Cape plumbago. A huge terracotta urn overflows with trailing ivy-leaf pelargoniums at the corner of the forecourt, marking the entrance to the main house. The forecourt is paved with loose stones and sunken, with retaining walls of rough stone marking the boundary to a lawn area with an assortment of shrubs, flowering apricot and cherries. Another massive date palm with a drinking trough for dogs at its base rises high above the roofline at the start of another garden path leading to a second entrance, and farther up the slope of the lawn is a younger specimen. Sporting a healthy crown of fronds, it seems to erupt like a fountain from a gap in a grove of bamboo that screens a group of three old water

cisterns in which the family kept goldfish. These serve as a reminder of the relative luxury of the new establishment at Les Collettes. The Renoirs had water piped from the bottom of this steep hill to the top. In former days the inhabitants of the old farmhouse had to walk down to the river Cagne to take a wash, and watering the livestock and crops had entailed manoeuvring cumbersome water barrels about on the steep and rough ground. Renoir's garden had every chance of flourishing thanks to the convenience of up-to-date garden hoses and the abundance of water.

An archway on the terrace of the main house is outlined with the early blooms of a climbing rose. Potted papyrus (left) grows in shady parts of the garden.

CHAPTER IV

THE ORCHARDS, VINEYARDS AND VEGETABLE GARDENS

'In my father's day . . . everyone had their own
vegetable garden, their chickens and rabbits.
Living was not dear, taxes were low and the natives travelled
about their business on donkeys, unhurried, never
wearing out the animals, the land or
themselves.'   *Jean Renoir*

Right Aline Renoir had charge of the extensive vegetable gardens and orchards. Here, in autumn, peach trees overhang rows of blue-green Savoy cabbages. The shamrock-like plants are wild oxalis. Straw-coloured oat grasses grow below the terrace.

Previous pages:
Left View along one of the terraces, with a crop of lettuce in the foreground and tomato plants supported on poles above a planting of haricot (pole) beans.
Right Vines at Cagnes (*c.*1908) shows a vineyard cradled in a sun-drenched valley, framed by the branches of olive trees.

Below Ripe olives, gathered and pressed, produced Les Collettes' own olive oil.

It is difficult to imagine today that Les Collettes was so self-sufficient an entity in Renoir's time. The goat pens, rabbit hutches and chicken house that were once so important to the economy of the household are all gone, though their foundations remain. The grassy terraces that descend the slope in a curve – rather like the levels in a Roman amphitheatre – in Renoir's day were intensively cultivated with flowers and vegetables. Characteristic of steep slopes all around the Mediterranean, these terraces have been in existence for hundreds of years, buttressed with low stone walls to prevent erosion and to preserve moisture in the soil. Now they are lawns. The Renoirs had glasshouses and cold frames to provide fresh produce all winter, and to raise cuttings and seedlings of flowering plants

Peaches and Grapes (1911). The gardens were a source of fresh fruit and vegetables for the table but also provided Renoir with subjects for his still-life studies.

for bedding out in various parts of the gardens. Carnations and roses were also grown under glass, so that all year round the house could be filled with fresh flowers. And season after season the orchards yielded their respective crops of olives, dessert fruit and flowers.

A short cut from the forecourt of the main house to the stairway leads down into the courtyard of the old farmhouse, and is marked by a narrow corridor of euonymus. This is a good route to the terraced area beyond the farmhouse, still cultivated to produce grapes, cherries, peaches, plums, apricots, almonds and figs. Jacques Renoir remembers as a boy finding a tree in this part of the garden that bore both oranges and lemons, a feat achieved by skilfully grafting a lemon on to an orange tree. Today only the stump remains, for the spectacular tree eventually succumbed to disease.

Behind the farmhouse is a productive vegetable garden – though today smaller in scale than when Renoir lived on the property. He not only enjoyed consuming fresh produce but also included many subjects from the vegetable garden and orchards in his still lifes. There are wonderful small paintings of this period: luscious red strawberries piled on a crisp white cloth, so vivid that you feel you could almost reach into the picture to touch them; there are paintings of melons and tomatoes, aubergines (eggplants), oranges, apples, lemons, onions and figs

Bitter orange trees were planted close to the house.

Right A bed of globe
artichokes with handsome
silvery leaves.

Below The large globular
flower buds and the tender
heart of the artichoke are
delicious when cooked.

Above A cauliflower grows
with health and vitality in
the fertile clay loam.

Every day Renoir would choose something, maybe just one apple or an orange, to
make a tiny vignette. There was also an enormous plot devoted to globe
artichokes. Artichoke plants require a permanent bed of rich soil and need to be
spaced well apart, so plenty of room was allocated to them at Les Collettes. They
grew well in the relatively frost-free climate of Cagnes, and fresh young artichoke
buds feature in several paintings.

A few of the old crops are still grown. Depending on the season, lettuce and
cabbage are cultivated in regimented blocks; broad (fava) beans and haricot
(pole) beans still clamber up bamboo-cane supports, and a large potato patch
yields an abundance of red-skinned tubers from the fertile humus-rich soil.
Clumps of herbs are planted randomly — dill, borage, thyme and nasturtiums
(*Tropaeolum majus*). The nasturtiums, used for salads, self-seed and grow with
wild abandon. Elsewhere in the garden, overhanging a wall, is a pepper tree
(*Schinus molle*) — a little tree, native to Peru, with an elegant, weeping habit. Not
a true member of the pepper family (its little coral-red berries have a juniper
flavour), it is widely grown in the Mediterranean for use in cooking.

Left View showing a storeroom and a crop of broad (fava) beans — the first vegetable to appear in spring — supported by bamboo poles.

Above White onions from Renoir's garden.

Below A harvest of radishes, variety 'French Breakfast'.

Between the farmhouse and the vegetable garden is a cluster of toolsheds and storerooms. There was no mechanization in Renoir's day: work was done by hand with fork, spade, hoe and rake in the vegetable garden, and the ground was generously fertilized with good home-grown manure and leaf mould. Much of the produce from the orchards and vegetable gardens was preserved for winter use or sold locally. Grapes were dried, as were apricots; lemons, oranges and tangerines would remain on the trees all winter, so that even lemons would become deliciously sweet; onions and garlic were hung up in strings, and root crops were dug up and stored in a clamp, buried under a mound of soil which would keep them fresh for months.

Grapevines display freshly unfurled bright green leaves in early spring along one of the terraces at Les Collettes. The vines flower in early summer and bear dessert-quality grapes by autumn. In Renoir's day, Aline cultivated a much larger vineyard on the property – grapes were a crop she particularly cherished since her family were vintners.

Les Collettes, like other country properties, was run as a self-sufficient smallholding. At first old Catherine and her son Paul continued to live at the farmhouse. Later, two families of gardeners stayed there and cultivated the extensive orchards, vineyards and vegetable gardens from which the household was supplied. As was the custom, in exchange for accommodation the families were expected to keep the land productive, but were not paid; instead they could sell surplus produce in the local markets as a means of earning income. The gardener Baptistin recalled an occasion when his father felt the family needed extra food over Christmas and appealed to Renoir for some money. Renoir was surprised at the request, and offered the man two of his paintings instead. The offer was turned down flat. 'Baptistin cannot eat the paintings', declared his father. Flabbergasted, Renoir kept the paintings and instead provided the necessary financial assistance.

Some of the crops at Les Collettes were produced on a commercial scale. In spring the orange blossoms were harvested for the scent factories at Grasse twenty miles away. Young women from the village would fan out through the trees picking the delicate, waxy white blooms and dropping them into wicker baskets. The fragrance released during the harvest was almost intoxicating and would carry for miles. Renoir liked to sit in his chair in the shade of his lime (linden) tree and look down on the spectacle. He not only loved the heady aroma, but enjoyed watching the dexterity of the young women. The blossoms were then taken by donkey cart to Grasse, where the fragrant oils would be distilled from them to perfume soap and scent.

In winter the ripened olives would be transported to an olive press in the village, where they were pressed to produce olive oil. With the first pressing, the Renoir family would come back to Les Collettes for a ceremonial tasting. Renoir liked to eat some of the syrupy first pressing spread on warm toast with a sprinkling of salt. It is said that he could distinguish the taste of oil from his own trees from that of others, which he regarded as inferior in flavour.

Les Collettes also had its own small vineyards along the terraces. The vines here produced wine of only modest quality, but the grapes were good to eat. Grapes generally grow well in the region: low rainfall is rarely a problem since the roots of the grapevine can grow downwards as much as 9 metres/30 feet — sometimes spreading three times farther still — and many of the best vineyards flourish in arid locations. The vineyards at Les Collettes were Madame Renoir's province. She had been brought up among vineyards: her father had been a wine grower at Essoyes, a village on the border between the two great wine-producing regions, Champagne and Burgundy, and Renoir had for many years owned a studio next to the farmhouse there. The Charigot household at Essoyes displayed a down-to-earth attitude to life, evidently attaching greater importance to the art of pruning and training vines and earning a livelihood from the land than to the business of the artist. It is said that paintings Renoir left with his wife's family were used to roof rabbit hutches. Her relatives thought that anything that came with such apparent facility could not possibly have any value.

Grape skins, on a terrace, will decompose and return nourishment to the soil.

A pile of autumn leaves, collected in a concrete bin, have been left to decay. The resulting leaf mould will be used to enrich the beds and borders.

Above Renoir and Aline pose together in the studio. When asked by Ambroise Vollard whether the land afforded a good income from its produce, Aline replied: 'Well, if Renoir were younger we could work the property together. But I suppose we have done better to rely on his painting.'

Right A jewel-like carpet of red poppies, yellow mustard and white daisies.

Below Nasturtiums flower freely among papyrus.

Jean Renoir wrote that, at heart, his mother remained a peasant all her life. She liked a country atmosphere and was a thoroughly practical and resourceful woman. Her life at Les Collettes centred on looking after her husband and his daily painting regimen. Renoir would decide from day to day whether to paint a model, a landscape or a still life. Once he had a brush firmly grasped in his disfigured fingers, he would keep to the same one and wash it out in turpentine between colours; although frail, he did not use a maulstick to steady his hand. Madame Renoir, jovial and supportive, played the role of his assistant. She prepared his palette, pressed and flattened his tubes of colour ready for use, and at the end of the painting session cleaned his brush and made ready the studio in the main house or the wooden one in the olive grove for the next day. Sometimes she helped him play a cup-and-ball game to revive his fingers between sittings. She would do the cooking by herself on days when Renoir 'borrowed' her maid to pose for him.

Everything revolved around Renoir: he was master of his universe, and although he was autocratic he was usually pleasant and mild-mannered — unlike Monet, who was given to fits of anger and violence, throwing tantrums when things did not go right or when the family got on his nerves. Once Renoir was settled at his easel he was good-humoured and content, despite the irritation the pain of his rheumatism caused him.

But little escaped his discerning eye, and anything involving the garden needed his approval, to the extent that the gardeners would even ask his permission to cut the grass. In such matters Renoir's fastidiousness rivalled that of Monet's, though it arose from a completely different philosophy. Monet had his elaborately planted garden groomed to create the compositions he had in mind: he even had a gardener whose principal duty was to keep his pond clean and ensure that there was enough separation between the clumps of waterlilies to enable reflections of the pond margin and sky to be seen clearly between the floating islands of foliage. While Monet sought to conquer nature and mould the landscape to his ideal, Renoir on the other hand strove to keep Les Collettes from being over-planted, to maintain the status quo and conserve nature's own patient handiwork. He liked the grass to grow long so that it formed decorative seed-heads and created special effects with the light; when one of the gardeners asked permission to weed a path, Renoir responded tersely, 'What weeds?'

View showing part of Renoir's vegetable garden, with old olive trees descending the slope. This section of the garden is now cultivated by René and Gisèle Nicolaï, caretakers who harvest the crops for their own use.

Comparing the gardens of Renoir and Monet, art historian John House observed: 'Almost like Monet, who built his water garden as his ideal pictorial subject in his late years, Renoir would construct at Les Collettes a physical world which would fulfil his pictorial vision. But it was quite different in two crucial ways: Monet built his anew, to his own aesthetic specifications, while Renoir's was old, preserved as an ideal vision of past society; and Monet's was an elaborately cultivated garden, conceived as an object of his solitary contemplation, whereas Renoir's view of nature necessarily implied the human presence, which the olives and the farm evoke so richly.'

Whenever Monet went away from Giverny on a trip he left pages of detailed notes for his gardeners. Renoir was happy to let Aline supervise the plantings at Les Collettes, he merely insisted that the garden elements that underpinned his romantic vision were retained. Madame Renoir skilfully balanced all these demands. Under her direction the impoverished soil was cultivated and fertilized; the olives were watered during dry spells and pruned just enough to remove dead limbs and maintain a pleasing shape – but not too much, for fear of distressing Renoir, who relished their wild appearance. The existing orange trees were manured and she helped to plant hundreds more citrus trees. She collected eggs and gathered produce from the garden, tied back the roses, reminded the gardeners when to plant seeds, order bulbs and divide artichokes, and took care of a hundred more of the daily tasks involved in running such a large household.

Aline Renoir was a wonderful cook: she was not only well versed in her native cooking – which drew on the celebrated cuisines of both Burgundy and Champagne – but had taken the trouble to learn many Provençal dishes, and became renowned throughout the art community for her delicious meals. A favourite dish of the household was cassoulet, made with ham and fresh produce

Above Bright red hot peppers bring colour to the vegetable garden in autumn.

Below Rows of lush green Swiss chard housed in cold frames.

Left Strawberries (1908) is an example of Renoir's passion for 'sonorous' red. Much of his work at Les Collettes is characterized by the 'rosy glow' evident in this small canvas.

Above A cluster of fig leaves, glistening with drops of rain, in the orchard at Les Collettes.

Right A plum tree heavily laden with its summer bounty of succulent red fruit.

from the garden: home-grown tomatoes, garlic, bay leaves and haricot (pole) beans – 'real beans grown like vines in strong soil; not the kind you grow in a field', reported Jean Renoir.

The most famous of her new dishes was bouillabaisse made from fish freshly caught at Cros-de-Cagnes, garlic, red peppers, fennel, potatoes, leeks, onions, tomatoes and fresh herbs, all grown at Les Collettes, with pinches of saffron added. Local fish and a mixture of fresh garden vegetables were also served with aïoli, the local mayonnaise made with egg yolks, olive oil and a vast quantity of garlic. Sometimes one of the villagers would bring little thrushes caught among the vines, and Madame Renoir would cook them on skewers over a honeysuckle fire. Potatoes would be baked in their jackets over hot ashes, and chestnuts in the same way. In season there would be fresh fruit – strawberries, figs, tangerines, oranges, apricots, plums and peaches. Like many good cooks, Aline put on a considerable amount of weight.

There were plenty of visitors to enjoy Aline's cooking at Les Collettes – long-standing friends Renoir had made while living in lower Cagnes. Paul Cézanne, son of the famous painter, came to live on the adjacent property and was a frequent visitor. Henri Matisse and Pierre Bonnard came to see Renoir, even though he disliked their paintings; Matisse was almost moved to tears by the extent of Renoir's deformities. Renoir also disliked Auguste Rodin's sculptures – which were not soft and flowing enough for his taste – but he welcomed Rodin to Les Collettes, and used a delay in Rodin's departure (caused by a car breakdown) to dash off a portrait of his guest in red chalk in less than an hour. Renoir's old friend Monet came to stay on a long visit in the winter of 1909 and was photographed in the olive orchard.

There were regular visits from picture dealers. Durand-Ruel, who made a great number of Impressionist painters wealthy by exhibiting their work internationally, was a frequent visitor. He organized many Renoir exhibitions, including one in New York in 1914 which was devoted entirely to his work. And in June of the same year, three of Renoir's pictures entered the Louvre as part of the bequest of Comte Isaac de Camondo.

Still Life with Apples and Almonds (n.d.), showing fruits gathered from the trees, is today exhibited in the main house. Despite the painting's title, the large fruit are in fact peaches.

Despite Renoir's ill-health, it was a happy household. The Renoirs' youngest son Coco would spend hours playing in the garden. Occasionally, if suitably bribed, he would consent to pose for his elderly father. He was a handsome child, and there are several wonderful paintings of him, for Renoir was incomparable as a painter of children. Renoir's eldest son Pierre was away from Les Collettes most of the time training to be an actor. The middle son Jean was sent to a boarding school he disliked intensely; he was withdrawn when in his teens and was then able to spend some time at home observing the routines and occurrences at Les Collettes and storing the memories and impressions that he would later draw on for his published memoir *Renoir, My Father.*

When the weather permitted, the family would sit out on the terrace in the evening under the big lime (linden) tree, and watch the fishermen at Cros-de-Cagnes sailing back to port with their catch of sardines. Renoir would amuse himself smoking a cigarette and, his son Jean recalled, was always the first to spot a boat, so keen was his eyesight. Then, after a game of draughts or dominoes with Aline, he would go early to bed. Vollard commented, 'He was afraid to stay up late in case it affected his work the next day. All his life painting was his one pleasure and his only recreation.'

CHAPTER

V

THE MAIN HOUSE
THE FINAL YEARS

'As his body dwindled, the soul in him seemed to grow
stronger continually and to express itself with more
radiant ease.' *Henri Matisse*

Above A chair in the drawing room is upholstered in a rose-patterned fabric which matches the room's paper border.

Previous pages:
Left View of the main house with white-flowered yuccas edging the path.
Right Roses in a Blue-and-White Vase (*c*.1915) shows an informal arrangement of roses and anemones.

Below The Empire sofa with its swan's neck design.

Today the main house at Les Collettes is a museum, a testimony to how Renoir and his family lived. The small entrance hall leads into a sunny living room with a polished red-tiled floor, furnished in essentially the same way as in Renoir's day. There is an Empire sofa, and chairs upholstered in a rich fabric of roses which matches the borders on the wallpaper. None of the furniture has sharp projecting corners. Renoir was extremely protective of his boisterous young sons. Fearful of their falling and hurting themselves and experiencing the same kind of disabilities he had suffered since his cycling accident, he took the precaution of seeing that there were no sharp corners anywhere in the house, even on tables, chairs and fireplaces.

Dominating the living room is Renoir's *The Bathers* (see page 42) – a version of his famous painting of the same title, now in the Philadelphia Museum of Art. Several art historians believe that this canvas was begun around 1884, abandoned, and then completed later (*c*.1901/2). Also on display in this room is an assortment of family photographs and paintings of the property done by other artists, particularly Renoir's friend Albert André.

The living room leads into the light airy dining room which has large French windows on two sides. It has a polished parquet floor and a traditional glass-fronted country dresser on which are displayed earthenware plates with a plum motif designed and painted by Coco, who grew up to enjoy success as a ceramist.

Both these rooms would have had vases filled with Aline's spectacular flower arrangements. All the models who lived with the family developed an interest in flower arranging, and could quickly conjure up an artistic display for Renoir to paint. 'Painting flowers is a form of relaxation,' he would say. 'I don't need the concentration that I have to have when I'm faced with a model.' He also soon discovered that flower paintings were much the easiest to sell. De Caen anemones were a favourite subject for his paintings, and these anemones still flourish at Les Collettes – red, white, blue, purple and pink, often bicoloured, with contrasting black centres.

Renoir also loved the bedding-type dahlias with rounded flower heads on bushy, succulent plants. With their reds, pinks, yellows and oranges, purples and whites, they reminded him so much of the old-fashioned flower gardens of Montmartre. In the Mediterranean climate they die back in winter but regenerate from tubers the following spring to flower in summer and autumn. Madame

Left View of the dining room from the drawing room.

Left A large dresser in the dining room supports a display of plates decorated by Coco.

A view through the stairwell
window captures the
autumnal glow of a
strawberry tree in full fruit.

Left The stairway from the ground floor to the first floor with a bust of Renoir's eldest son, Pierre.

Renoir often used them in her arrangements. Renoir loved both the fragrance and the colours of carnations and, since Cagnes was a centre for year-round carnation growing to provide cut flowers for the florist trade, it was natural for the Renoirs to cultivate them in their range of glasshouses on the terraces below, and to enjoy them about the house. Then there were the simpler flowers that also appealed to Renoir – black-centred scarlet corn poppies (*Papaver rhoeas*) which grew wild among the oat grasses, and white marguerite daisies with yellow centres.

On the ground floor of the main house is the kitchen. It is here that Madame Renoir would have presided over the big wood- and charcoal-burning cast-iron range in which her excellent meals were produced. The servants' quarters and guest rooms are also on this floor. A polished wooden staircase leads up to the next floor. Halfway up the landing is a bust of Renoir's eldest son Pierre, which Renoir made in his last years. The window here looks out on to the shiny dark green foliage of a Killarney strawberry tree (*Arbutus unedo*). In late autumn this is studded with both creamy yellow flowers and edible strawberry-like fruits, while the leathery toothed leaves turn to russet colours.

Below Dahlias (c.1890). These flowers reminded Renoir of the gardens of Montmartre and were often arranged around the house.

Renoir's studio as visitors see it today is little changed from the day he died. His wheelchair, folding table and easel are arranged as he had them, with natural light flooding the room through the arched window.

Renoir's studio upstairs has the aura of a shrine, for it is large, with a high ceiling, and there is a tendency for visitors to talk in whispers when walking through it, as if to avoid disturbing the artist. The studio has a floor-to-ceiling arched picture window overlooking the front lawn with its massive date palm and, beyond, the soft silvery green crowns of the olive trees. Renoir's wheelchair with its rattan seat and back stands in front of the easel, on which a copy of one of his rose paintings is propped. Nearby on a table is a real bouquet of roses. The room contains an arabesque couch with a red canopy, and various props that his models or children would dress up in while posing.

Renoir's wheelchair and his painting paraphernalia — artist's palette, wooden

Above The studio window overlooks trees on the lawn.

Left Renoir's folding table and artist's materials. 'Without paints in tubes there would have been no Cézanne, no Monet, no Sisley, no Pissarro, nothing of what journalists were to call Impressionism', declared Renoir.

Below The bust of *Venus Victrix* in the studio was a preliminary study for Renoir's famous sculpture.

paintbox, brushes, paints, folding table and stacks of canvases — evoke his presence in the studio. You can imagine him at work. The table has a canvas top to support the jar of aromatic linseed oil used for thinning paint, a blue rag for wiping slender sable brushes clean and a wooden cup for holding brushes. The delicate bristles at the tips of the brushes have long since fallen out, and the paint labels are faded, but the silvery lead tubes of oil paints are intact, as on the day Renoir died — some of them plump and hardly touched, others squeezed flat to use every precious drop of paint; one even has a lump of pigment congealed around a crack below the neck of the tube.

When his sons came to sort out Renoir's paintings after his death, they found

Right Renoir's bathroom is stark and simple. The deep bath allowed him to soak up to his neck and relieve his rheumatic pain.

Below This humorous tile in the bathroom was painted by Coco and shows his mother using the bidet.

numerous tiny canvases 'without stretchers and in piles of ten, twenty, crammed into old trunks. Many had several pictures on the same canvas: a sugar bowl with flowers, two red mullet, an orange, some anemones, a torso, a little face.' There were landscapes of Les Collettes with faces of his models, or anemones or roses upside down in the wide margins around them. Some of his last paintings of Les Collettes look almost slapdash – painted with flickering elongated strokes where no tree or flower is recognizable, almost as though a whirlwind had swept through the scene. There were also some large compositions – 'flowery breasts, leaping children, the light in the sky, beautiful bodies of girls', all glowing with warmth and the expression of Renoir's increasing delight in a sculptural form.

Renoir used this studio a good deal when the family first moved to Les Collettes, but he tended to find it bleak and a little isolated upstairs next to the bedrooms, away from the hubbub of household activity. He preferred the ambience of his little shed among the olive trees, and right up until his very last days would ask to be carried or wheeled there to paint. Just sometimes, when his rheumatism was particularly bad, he would settle for working in the house studio.

Renoir's bedroom is next to Aline's – each with sunny windows and lace

curtains. A balcony off Aline's room provides spectacular views of the Mediterranean sea and the Maritime Alps, capped in snow for much of the year. There are smaller bedrooms for the children, and a bathroom which is starkly white except for a humorous ceramic painted tile by Coco showing his mother using the bidet. A third level – a false basement opening on to the hillside terrace – has rooms for storage and a ceramics workshop, converted into a caretaker's apartment.

The main building now houses ten of Renoir's paintings: there are landscapes showing parts of the garden – *The Avenue Under the Trees, Landscape at Les Collettes, The Farmhouse at Les Collettes* (see page 27); there are portraits, possibly painted in the upstairs studio, a still life of peaches and almonds (page 79), and several nude studies. After a recent visit to the house, Michael Peppiatt

Landscape at Les Collettes (1918). The countryside around Cagnes is framed by two old olive trees. The painting forms part of the exhibition of original work in the main house.

Above A wild flower nestles in the gnarled bark of an olive tree.

Right The main door of the old farmhouse opens on to the olive orchard.

Below Delicate markings inside the throat of a pink-flowering angel's trumpet.

wrote in the *Architectural Digest* magazine: 'Today the garden is as present inside the house at Les Collettes as outside, since two of the best paintings hanging there memorably convey the idyllic surroundings. In those paintings Renoir so heightens the luminosity on each fragment of leaf, bark and soil that the eye first recoils as if from a burst of real sunlight.'

Aline Renoir in 1915, the year of her death.

The declaration of war in August 1914 marked the end of an era at Les Collettes and the prelude to tragedy in the Renoir family. It was not Renoir's first experience of war: as a young man in 1870 he had enlisted in the cavalry during the Franco-Prussian war. He was never, however, sent to the front, as he contracted dysentery, an illness which left his face permanently gaunt.

Pierre and Jean both enlisted. In the following year both were wounded. Jean was hit in the thigh; there was a possibility of gangrene, and for some time it was feared that the leg would have to be amputated. Madame Renoir, who suffered from diabetes and was already not in the best of health, travelled the length and breadth of France to visit her sons in their military hospitals. Through her intervention Jean's leg was saved, but the stress and anxiety Aline experienced during the trip brought on her final illness. She died shortly after returning to Les Collettes, on 27 June 1915, and was buried at Essoyes.

Aline had been Renoir's constant companion and helpmate for more than thirty years. He had depended on her to run his household and organize his life, and he sorely missed her.

The war made life at Les Collettes isolated as well as lonely by depriving Renoir of his driver. A few years earlier Renoir had acquired a Renault car and promoted Baptistin to chauffeur. At first the car had been left at the bottom of the hill and Renoir had been carried to and from it by Baptistin and La Grande Louise – one of his models, who was a tall, strong girl. Eventually Renoir decided that this voyage by sedan chair was too precarious, and he had the road made up to the top of the hill. Now, with war, there was no one to drive him.

Each day became an agonizing ritual as he dressed and ate and prepared to paint. Renoir began especially to dread the dark evenings: 'I find the last hours of the day quite interminable.' Gone was the time when he could while away the hours after supper playing draughts with Aline. To escape from this solitude, he

Renoir at Les Collettes, 1917-18.

Jean Renoir with his father, 1916.

Renoir in his studio with Andrée Heuschling, who became his favourite model after Gabrielle left the household to marry. Andrée – or Dédée as she was nicknamed – married Renoir's second son, Jean.

rented an apartment in Nice where he stayed when the days grew short. He did not participate in the activities or night life of Nice, but he felt comforted to have the sights and sounds of a busy cosmopolitan city surrounding him during the dark evening hours.

After the Armistice Jean returned to Cagnes to live with his father and found the house 'sinister'. The orange trees and the vineyards were almost wild. 'It was as if people, trees, everything mourned my mother. The car was garaged and covered with a thick layer of dust.'

Vollard recalled Renoir from one of his visits after Aline's death. 'He seemed discouraged. "I no longer want to paint. I'm no good at anything any more." He had closed his eyes with such an air of defeat. I went out into the garden, feeling that my presence was unwanted. A few minutes later La Grande Louise was calling me: "The Master wants you in his studio."' Vollard found Renoir at his easel, radiant. 'He was struggling to paint some dahlias. "Look, Vollard. Isn't this just as brilliant as a Delacroix battle scene? I think that I've really discovered the secret of painting . . . How I wish I could live just long enough to paint a masterpiece."'

Admirers still made the pilgrimage to see Renoir. The area he lived in now attracted a number of painters. Chaïm Soutine and Moise Kisling were living in lower Cagnes. After Matisse came from Nice to see him, he described how he found Renoir: 'The joints of his fingers were all immense, calloused, horribly distorted . . . and he still did all his best work . . . As his body dwindled, the soul in him seemed to grow stronger continually and to express itself with more radiant ease.'

After Gabrielle left the household Renoir discovered a beautiful red-haired young model, Andrée Heuschling, known as Dédée. One of Renoir's last paintings of this period was another study of *The Bathers* (1918), now in the Musée d'Orsay, for which Andrée was a model. This lyrical painting with its warm glowing colours differs greatly from the much more realistic treatment of the first famous version created during his 'Harsh' period. Jean fell for Andrée Heuschling, married her and rhapsodized: 'Along with the roses, which grew almost wild at Les Collettes, and the great olive trees with their silvery reflections, Andrée was one of the vital elements that helped Renoir to interpret on his canvas the tremendous cry of love he uttered at the end of his life.'

The handsome, timid Amadeo Modigliani came to Les Collettes to see Renoir with a friend in 1918, just two years before his own death. Renoir, now seventy-seven, had never heard of Modigliani, nor of his paintings portraying slender women with narrow elongated faces and doleful expressions, but made an effort to give him a courteous welcome. Modigliani was shown into the living room where Renoir was sitting quietly after a day's work in the studio among the olive trees. He had some of his pictures taken down from the wall so that Modigliani could examine them more closely. Presently Renoir broke the silence by asking, 'You brought me one of your canvases to show me, didn't you? Let me see it.' The painting was produced and inspected, but Renoir, obviously displeased, commented, 'Do you paint with a feeling of joy? . . . You should paint with joy, young man. Paint with the same joy you feel when making love to a woman. You should caress your canvases, caress them for a long time. I spend days and days stroking the buttocks of the nudes in my pictures before I finish them.' Modigliani,

Lime Tree and Farmhouse (*c.*1919). This view of the farmhouse and the lime (linden) tree at Les Collettes was painted, in the year of Renoir's death, from the side of the terrace at the rear of the main house.

Anemones (*c*.1915). Blooming in early spring throughout the Mediterranean, anemones have large poppy-like flowers with a conspicuous mound of powdery black stamens at their centre. A bouquet of roses in his bedroom, a painting of anemones on his easel, Renoir's last word as he lapsed into unconsciousness before death was 'flowers'.

appalled by Renoir's remarks, grasped the door-handle, face twitching, and blurted: 'I, Monsieur, do not like buttocks.'

In these last years Renoir no doubt enjoyed the homage of young painters, though he found it somewhat difficult to come to terms with his fame. He was offered the Legion of Honour but anguished over whether or not to accept it for fear that it would upset his old friend, Monet. The day before he died he said 'I am still making progress'.

Renoir was taken ill in November but seemed to recover. At the beginning of December he suddenly felt worse, and a lung infection was diagnosed. In his studio he had been painting a bunch of anemones. He asked for his paintbox and brushes to be brought into the bedroom.

Renoir died peacefully in the early hours of 3 December 1919, in Aline's old bedroom. He was seventy-eight. The art critic Félix Fénéon described how he took his farewell of his friend: 'In his room . . . at Les Collettes, whose windows open on to the trees and sea, he lies on a bed that is covered with his favourite flowers, a bower of yellow and pink roses. Face pure and emaciated, but not hard; mouth half-open.'

'His life and work were prolonged in this land of blue skies and sunshine', art critic Gustave Geffroy wrote by way of eulogy. 'There he was able to breathe and paint, to contemplate its greenness and flowers, its sky and water. There on the doorstep or at the bottom of his garden was all that is beautiful and smiling in nature for Renoir's use.'

With a large umbrella to shade his sensitive skin and reduce glare on the canvas, the aged, ailing Renoir paints in the garden at Les Collettes, a paintbrush bandaged to his hand.

POSTCRIPT

◆

After Renoir's death in 1919, the entire estate was willed to his youngest son, Claude, since he was only nineteen years old, while his two elder brothers were married and had homes of their own. More than 400 original paintings were found in the house and, according to Renoir's will, they had to be divided equally among the boys; the local police chief administered the division.

Claude lived at Les Collettes until 1960 when it was acquired by the town of Cagnes and the general council of the Maritime Alps as a museum to Renoir. Two pieces of land were sold privately – a section at the bottom of the property and another section at the top, across from the main road where Renoir had had a pottery kiln constructed for Claude. Otherwise, the property is essentially the same as in Renoir's day.

In the spring of 1988, Madame Suzanne Sauvaigo, Mayor of Cagnes, accompanied a mission to the United States. During a journey to Washington DC, Boston and New York, aided by the 'Vieilles Maisons Françaises' Association – a type of national trust interested in saving old French houses – a total of $50,000 was collected. This allowed a security system to be installed at the main house so that some choice pieces of original art by Renoir could be put on public display.

For the future, as more funds are realized, the town of Cagnes plans to restore the old farmhouse so that visitors can see inside, where an old documentary film showing Monet, Renoir and Degas at work will be screened. It is also hoped to restore more of the gardens by employing gardeners.

Les Collettes still needs funds for restoration. Anyone interested in making a donation should contact the mayor's office, Cagnes.

MAP OF FRANCE

—◆—

The map below shows major
towns as well as areas with
which Renoir, his family,
friends and fellow painters
were associated.

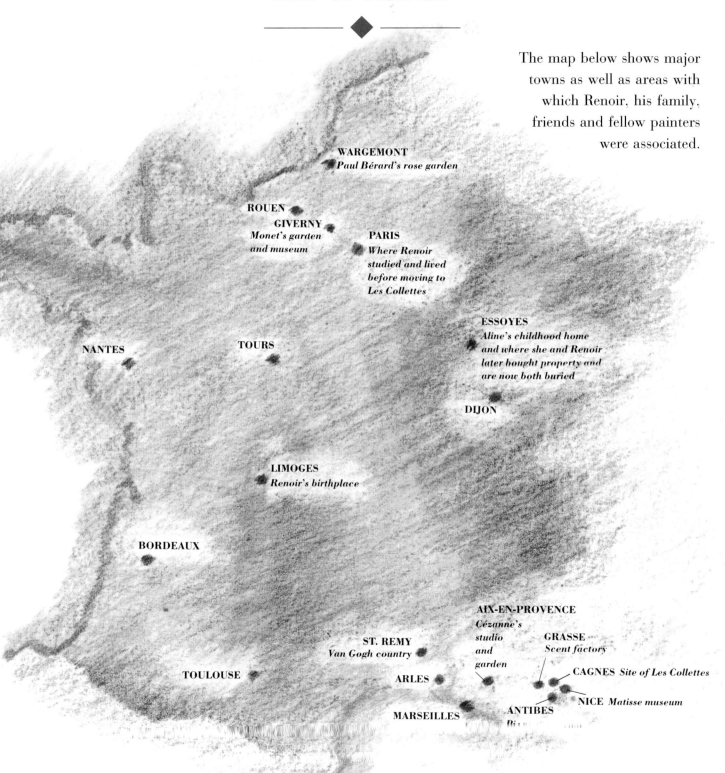

WARGEMONT
Paul Bérard's rose garden

ROUEN

GIVERNY
*Monet's garden
and museum*

PARIS
*Where Renoir
studied and lived
before moving to
Les Collettes*

ESSOYES
*Aline's childhood home
and where she and Renoir
later bought property and
are now both buried*

NANTES

TOURS

DIJON

LIMOGES
Renoir's birthplace

BORDEAUX

AIX-EN-PROVENCE
*Cézanne's
studio
and
garden*

GRASSE
Scent factory

ST. REMY
Van Gogh country

CAGNES *Site of Les Collettes*

TOULOUSE

ARLES

NICE *Matisse museum*

ANTIBES

MARSEILLES

PLANS OF THE GARDEN

◆

The keys to the buildings and garden features and to the trees and plants refer to both the elevation (below) and the garden plan (right).

ELEVATION
looking towards the farmhouse with the main house beyond

KEY TO ELEVATION AND GARDEN PLAN

Buildings and Garden Features
A Farmhouse
B Main house
C *Venus Victrix*
D Courtyard
E Site of Renoir's studio
F Gardener's cottage
G Terrace (of main house)
H Fish ponds
I Cistern
J Toolsheds/storerooms

K Pedestal (former site of *Venus Victrix*)
L Main entrance
M Lower entrance

Trees and plants
1 Olive grove
2 Umbrella pine grove
3 Palm trees
4 Vineyard
5 Lime (linden) tree
6 Olive trees

7 Bamboo grove
8 Oak grove
9 Cactus garden
10 Cypress trees
11 Shrubbery
12 Strawberry tree
13 Cherry tree
14 Orange trees
15 Citrus trees
16 Peach trees
17 Plum tree
18 Apricot tree

19 Loquats
20 Rose garden and citrus orchard
21 Pelargoniums
22 Irises
23 Oleanders
24 Wild flowers and oat grasses
25 Terraces
26 Vegetable garden
27 Artichokes
28 Lower garden

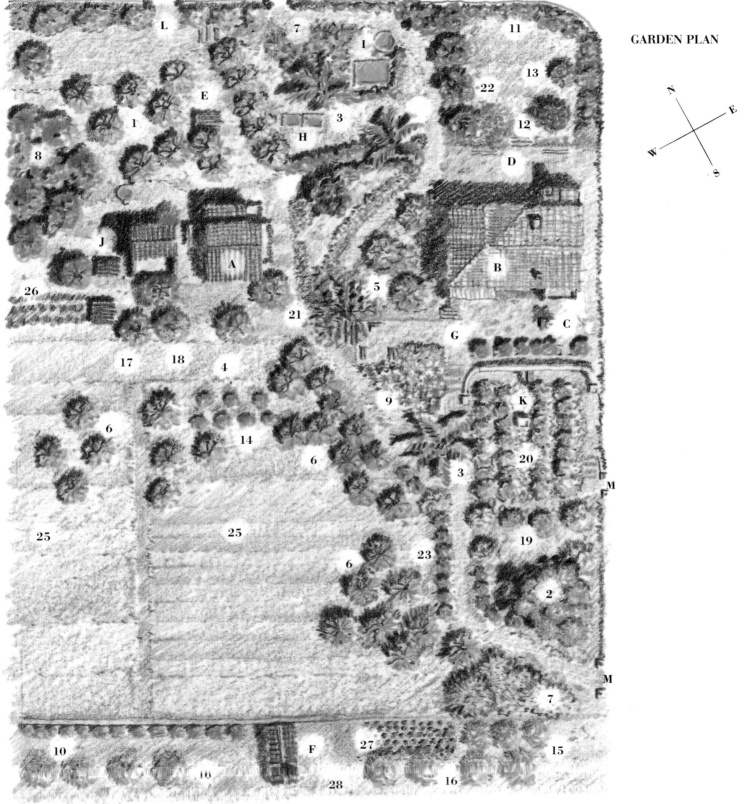

GARDEN PLAN

FORMAL BORDER

1 Ivy-leaf pelargoniums
2 Climbing roses
3 Shrub verbena
4 Canary Island date palm
5 Calamondin orange tree
6 Agapanthus (African lily)
7 Santolina (lavender cotton)
8 Angel's trumpet (datura)
9 *Venus Victrix*

INFORMAL BORDER

1 Juniper tree
2 Cypress tree
3 Pine tree
4 Climbing roses
5 Poppies
6 Irises
7 Ivy-leaf pelargonium
8 Soapwort
9 Carnations
10 Oat grasses
11 Daisies
12 Calendulas
13 Anchusa

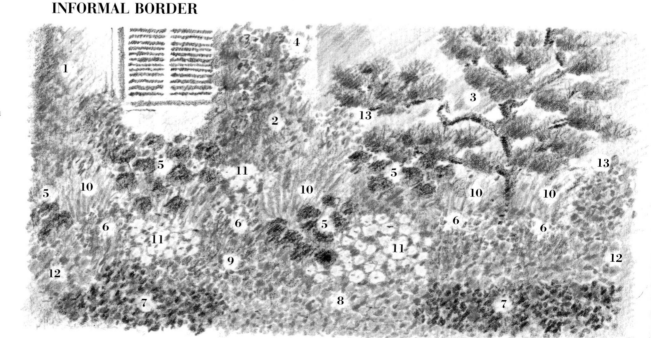

THE PLANTS

Following is a list of the principal ornamental plants and trees in Renoir's garden, some grown for cutting, others for garden display.

Agapanthus africanus (African lily, blue lily of the Nile)

Agave americana 'Variegata' (century plant)

Aloe species (aloe)

Anchusa azurea (blue anchusa)

Anemone De Caen (French anemone)

Arbutus unedo (strawberry tree)

Argyranthemum frutescens (Paris daisy, marguerite)

Bergenia cordifolia (heartleaf)

Beschorneria yuccoides (Mexican yucca)

Brugmansia species (angel's trumpet, datura)

Campsis grandiflora (trumpet creeper)

Canna × *generalis* (giant canna)

Carpobrotus edulis (Hottentot fig)

Cercis siliquastrum (redbud, Judas tree)

Cestrum aurantiacum (orange cestrum)

Chrysanthemum coronarium (crown daisy)

Cistus species (rock rose)

Citrus species (citrus – orange, lemon, lime, etc.)

Crataegus species (hawthorn)

Cupressus sempervirens (Italian cypress)

Cyperus papyrus (papyrus)

Cyphomandra crassicaulis, syn. *C. betacea* (tree tomato)

Dahlia hybrids (dahlia)

Dasylirion species (bear grass)

Dianthus caryophyllus (carnation)

Elaeagnus pungens (thorny elaeagnus)

Eucalyptus species (gum tree)

Euonymus species (spindle tree)

Felicia amelloides (kingfisher daisy)

Fuchsia 'Riccartonii' (fuchsia)

Gladiolus species and cultivars (gladiolus)

Hebe species and cultivars (shrubby veronica)

Hedera canariensis (Canary Island ivy)

Hemerocallis hybrids (day-lilies)

Hydrangea macrophylla (florist hydrangea)

Iris xiphium hybrids (Dutch iris)

Iris germanica hybrids (bearded iris)

Lantana camara (yellow sage, shrub verbena)

Lathyrus odoratus (sweet pea)

Lavandula angustifolia (common lavender)

Lavandula stoechas (French lavender)

Nerium oleander (oleander)

Olea europaea (European olive)

Opuntia species (prickly pear)

Papaver rhoeas (field poppy, corn poppy)

Parthenocissus tricuspidata 'Veitchii' (Boston ivy)

Passiflora incarnata (passion flower)

Pelargonium peltatum (ivy-leaf geranium)

Pericallis × *hybrida* (cineraria)

Philadelphus coronarius (mock orange)

Phoenix canariensis (Canary Island date palm)

Phyllostachys aureosulcata (yellow/golden groove bamboo)

Phytolacca americana (pokeweed)

Pinus pinea (umbrella pine)

Pittosporum tobira (fragrant pittosporum)

Polygala × *dalmaisiana* (sweet pea shrub)

Prunus species (ornamental cherry and plum)

Pyracantha coccinea (firethorn)

Ranunculus asiaticus (Persian buttercup)

Rhaphiolepis indica (Indian hawthorn)

Rosa banksiae 'Lutea' (Lady Banks's or Banksian rose)

Rosa 'Painter Renoir' (shrub rose)

Rosa, climbing varieties (climbing roses)

Rosmarinus cultivars (rosemary)

Santolina chamaecyparissus (lavender cotton)

Schinus molle (pepper tree)

Senecio bicolor cineraria (dusty miller)

Solanum rantonnetii (now correctly *Lycianthes rantonnetii*) (blue potato bush)

Syringa vulgaris (common lilac)

Tilia platyphyllos (broad-leaved lime/linden)

Trachycarpus fortunei (Chusan palm)

Tropaeolum majus (nasturtium)

Viburnum prunifolium (black haw)

Wisteria sinensis (wisteria)

Yucca species (yucca)

Zantedeschia aethiopica (arum or calla lily)

PHOTOGRAPHING LES COLLETTES

◆

I made three photographic trips to Les Collettes: first in early July under cloudless blue skies; again the following spring, when I had two rainy days during a week's stay, and finally in October, when days are shorter and the quality of the sunlight more muted. Using only natural light, I was seeking to capture the atmosphere of the place in compositions of varying kinds: overall views to help establish a sense of place; specific scenes such as views of the farmhouse, the olive trees and various planting schemes, and close-ups.

Red and yellow gaillardia mingle with nasturtiums.

I used an Olympus for the 35mm colour slides and a Rollei SLX to shoot larger-format 6×6cm/2¼×2¼in slides. I chose Ektachrome 64 professional colour transparency film: I prefer it to higher-speed films for its ability to render blue skies and the bright greens of a garden landscape faithfully, and also because I dislike the more grainy image created when faster films are enlarged.

I rarely used anything other than a standard lens. Les Collettes is spacious enough to make a wide-angle lens unnecessary, and I have an aversion to using telephoto lenses in gardens since they distort distances.

Using a tripod allowed me to shoot with small apertures such as f/11 and f/16 in order to achieve maximum depth of field. Except when shooting distant vistas, such as Haut-de-Cagnes crowned by the Château Grimaldi, I seldom took pictures at the infinity setting, but aimed to achieve needle-sharpness by focusing on something definite in the middle ground. I also tried to avoid taking pictures of scenery as a flat panorama, and often adjusted my position to find some element in the foreground to help frame my compositions.

It is amazing how a garden like Les Collettes changes from minute to minute when light and mood become an important part of the picture. Whenever the slightest change in the weather suggested a different lighting situation, I would head for the garden. Morning light seems to yield particularly good views, and the overcast days helped to accentuate flower colours. Though floral displays seem to last for weeks, a plant such as the yellow Lady Banks's rose will often seem to have a particular day when it is at its peak of perfection.

One of the most exhilarating aspects of garden photography is seeing a beautiful scene, photographing it and then finding it revealed on film even better than you remember it. This happens only rarely, because the eye tends to perceive images differently from the camera. Experience teaches us to recognize those occasions when a photograph can enhance what registers with the naked eye: some technical skill in handling the camera plus attention to creative composition can sometimes succeed in capturing them.

Renoir's garden is a more sophisticated beauty to photograph than, say, Monet's garden, with its lavish floral plantings and its preponderance of colour. The beauty in Renoir's garden is subtle – conveyed more in textural qualities than bright colour saturation, and in details easily overlooked in the grand scheme but brought into focus by the eye of the camera.

Yet some of the magic of Les Collettes will always elude the camera, and never be better conveyed than through the vision of Renoir's paintings.

The magical and at times almost supernatural aura of Renoir's garden is captured in this view of the olive grove at sunrise.

CHRONOLOGY OF RENOIR'S LIFE

1841 Pierre-Auguste Renoir born 25th February, Limoges.

1844 Family moves to Paris.

1854 Leaves school to become apprentice in porcelain factory.

1861 Studies at studio of Charles Gleyre, where he meets Monet, Sisley, Bazille and many other talented painters. Simultaneously follows course of studies at L'Ecole Impériale et Spéciale des Beaux-Arts.

1863 Enjoys company of Monet, Sisley and Bazille, painting in open air around Fontainebleau.

1864 Exhibits painting entitled *Esmeralda* at Salon of French Academy.

1865 Stays with Monet and Pissarro in the house of the painter Jules Le Coeur at Marlotte. With Sisley travels down Seine to Le Havre.

1866 Submissions to Salon refused.

1867 In spring, paints views of Paris with Monet.

1868 *Lise with an Umbrella* accepted by Salon.

1869 Works with Monet at Bougival; both paint at the island retreat of 'La Grenouillère'. Renews acquaintance with Cézanne, Manet, the writer Zola and photographer Nadar.

1870 War declared between France and Prussia. Enlists in cavalry, discharged after one year and paints in Paris. Monet moves to London to escape war where he meets art dealer Durand-Ruel. Monet later introduces him to Renoir.

1872 Lives near Monet at Argenteuil and renews contact with Caillebotte, wealthy patron of Impressionist movement. Durand-Ruel buys some of his work. Moves to Montmartre, lives in old mansion with overgrown garden. Paints prolifically.

1873 Exhibition of Impressionists known as 'Independents' ridiculed but Renoir praised for *The Theatre Box*.

1875 Rents studio in rue Cortot. With Monet, Sisley and Berthe Morisot, exhibits at Hôtel Drouot.

1876 Exhibits 15 paintings in Impressionist exhibition. Critical acclaim.

Coco up a tree at Les Collettes, 1910.

Pierre Renoir with his father in Paris, 1908.

Left Renoir, Aline and Coco at Essoyes, 1909.

1879   *Madame Charpentier and her Children* a huge success at Salon. Fame spreads. Becomes weekend guest of many wealthy Parisian families. Commissions for portraits.

1880   Begins work on *Luncheon of the Boating Party*. Aline Charigot, his future wife, is a model for the painting.

1881   Visits Algeria and later in the year, Italy.

1883   Durand-Ruel sponsors important exhibition of Renoir's work. Visits Channel Islands. With Monet goes to South of France and Italy, returning through Provence to visit Cézanne. Begins to veer away from Impressionism.

1884   Begins *The Bathers*.

1885   Aline gives birth to Renoir's first son, Pierre. Rents house in Normandy, near Giverny where Monet has now settled.

1886   First exhibition of Renoir's work in New York organized by Durand-Ruel.

1887   *The Bathers* receives critical acclaim at International Exhibition.

1888   Visits Cézanne. Suffers facial paralysis.

1890   Marries Aline Charigot, 14th April.

1892   Travels to Spain, visits Madrid and Seville.

1894   Caillebotte dies, leaving collection of Impressionist art to State. Birth of second son, Jean.

1895   Visits England.

1897   Buys farm at Essoyes, Aline's home village on the border of Burgundy and Champagne. Breaks arm in bike-riding accident. Later suffers severe attacks of rheumatism as a consequence.

1899   Death of Sisley in utter poverty.

1900   Awarded the Legion of Honour for his work as a painter.

1901   Third son, Claude (nicknamed Coco) born.

1902   Health deteriorates.

1903   Death of Pissarro.

1904   Moves with family to Cagnes for winter months.

1906   Death of Cézanne at Aix-en-Provence.

1907   Buys Les Collettes.

1908   Builds new house at Les Collettes; planting of gardens begins. Exhibition in New York.

1909   Visited by Monet.

1910   Exhibition of 35 paintings at Durand-Ruel's with works by Monet, Pissarro and Sisley. Visits Germany.

1911   Made Officer of the Legion of Honour.

1912   Exhibition of 58 portraits at Durand-Ruel's. Loses use of legs.

1914   Outbreak of First World War. Pierre and Jean enlist, both wounded. Exhibition in New York.

1915   Jean severely wounded. Aline dies, 27th June, in Nice.

1918   Matisse visits Les Collettes. Modigliani visits.

1919   Made Commander of the Legion of Honour. Dies 3rd December, aged 78, at Les Collettes. Body taken to Essoyes to be buried alongside Aline.

The main driveway at Les Collettes, 1913.

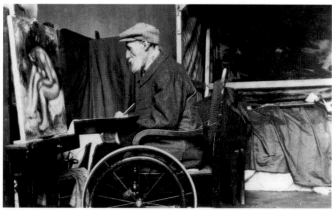

Renoir painting in his wheelchair, 1910.

GARDENS TO VISIT
IN THE SOUTH OF FRANCE

◆

The South of France, where Renoir spent his last years, is an area rich in public and private gardens – the list that follows includes some of the finest and most interesting. While every effort has been made to ensure accuracy of information, visitors are advised to check the opening times of the gardens.

Cézanne's house and garden, Aix-en-Provence.

AIX-EN-PROVENCE

Cézanne's Garden and Studio
Avenue Paul Cézanne. Open every day from 10am to noon and from 2pm to 5pm (6pm in summer). Tel: 42 21 06 53.
An informal garden, similar to Les Collettes. Restored by funds mainly from North American art patrons.

ANTIBES

Picasso Museum and Terrace Garden
Old Town of Antibes, Place Mariejol, 06600 Antibes. The museum and terrace garden is open every day (except Tuesdays, public holidays and throughout November) from 10am to noon and from 2pm to 6pm (3pm to 7pm in summer). Tel: 93 34 91 91

Roses Meilland Richardier
134 Boulevard Francis Meilland, BP 1225, 06600 Cap d'Antibes. Open during the first two weeks of February, April, June and November, except Saturdays, Sundays and public holidays. Admission by appointment.
4 hectares/10 acres with 24,000 square metres/29,000 square yards of greenhouses devoted to roses.

Villa Eilen Roc
Avenue Eilen Roc, 06600 Cap d'Antibes. Open Wednesdays from 1.30pm to 5pm except during French school holidays.
10 hectares/25 acres of typical Mediterranean vegetation, with melaleucas, parasol pines, Aleppo pines, palm trees, holm oaks, halophytic (salt-tolerant) plants. Garden transformed in 1930. Owned by the town of Antibes since 1982, its name is an anagram of the first name of the original owner's wife, Cornelie Loudon.

Villa Thuret
Chemin G. Raymond, BP 2078, 06606 Antibes. Public park. Open from 8.30am to 5.30pm, except Saturdays, Sundays and public holidays. Tel: 93 67 88 00. Admission free.
Arboretum of almost 3.5 hectares/9 acres with approximately 3000 species of trees and shrubs, mainly of subtropical origin, from: Australia, South Africa, Asia, Mexico, California, Canary Islands. State-owned since 1975 (donated by Gustave Thuret who created it in 1856).

BIOT

Le Chèvre d'Or
Groups of 25 to 30 admitted by appointment – preferably between the beginning of April and the end of June – approximately ten days in advance. Tel: 93 65 13 61. Admission free.
Garden created in 1950, property of Mrs Champin. Avenue of cypress trees, an orange grove, gardens devoted to the colours green, white and pink.

CAGNES

Château de Cagnes (known as Château Grimaldi)
Place du Château, Haut-de-Cagnes. Open every day except

Château de Cagnes.

Tuesdays from 10am to noon and from 2pm to 6pm (7pm in summer). Tel: 93 20 85 57. Entrance fee.
Renaissance patio with flowers and plants. Musée de l'olivier (olive industry museum). Fortified castle built at the end of the 13th century by Raynier Grimaldi, Admiral of France.

Les Collettes
Open every day except Tuesdays from 2pm to 5pm (10 Nov to 31 May); 10am to noon and from 2pm to 6pm (1 June to 14 October). Tel: 93 20 61 07. Entrance fee.
Renoir's garden from 1908 to 1919, now owned by the town of Cagnes. House contains paintings and sculpture by Renoir.

CANNES

Villa Domergue
Avenue de Fiesole. Formerly the 'Villa Fiesole'. Visits by appointment for groups. Tel: 93 83 92 59. Admission free.
Italian-style gardens, cascade, ponds, fountains, statues, aromatic plants. Tomb of J.G. Domergue and his wife, who lived in the villa from 1936 to 1962.

The following islands can be reached from Cannes by the Compagnie Este Chanteclair's regular ferry service from the Gare Maritime on the harbour, next to the Palais des Festivals.

Ile Saint Honorat
Private property, just south of Sainte Marguerite. Free access but visitors are requested to respect the religious life of the monks.
Nettle trees, magnolias, Judas trees, Aleppo pines, cypress and eucalyptus trees protect an undergrowth of thyme, cistus, genista, myrtle and rosemary. Traditional cultivation – as in the Middle Ages – of lavender which is sold on the island by the Sisters of Bethlehem.

Ile Sainte Marguerite
Admission free.
Nearly 120 hectares/300 acres of national forests and includes: holm oaks, Aleppo pines, parasol pines, maritime pines, cypresses, Australian eucalyptus trees, cedars, Judas trees, oleanders, false pepper plants; undergrowth of heather, lentiscus, arbutus. Flora clearly labelled along the botanic

pathway. Exceptionally beautiful avenue of eucalyptus trees, 400 metres/440 yards long, planted before the 1870 Franco-Prussian war. The main point of interest offered by the island's fortress is that it served as the prison in *The Man in the Iron Mask*.

EZE

Jardin Exotique
Rue du Château, Eze Village. Gardens open every day from 9am until noon and 2pm until sunset. Tel: 93 41 10 30. Entrance fee. Exotic plants: agaves, aloes, cacti. Fine panoramic views of the Mediterranean. Gardens created in 1950 on the ramparts of a fortified castle, destroyed in 1706.

GRASSE

Villa-Museum Fragonard and its Garden
23 Boulevard Fragonard. Municipal Museum. Open every day except Mondays and Tuesdays, 10am to 6pm. Tel: 93 36 01 61. 2500 square metres/3000 square yards with several century-old palm trees that survived the harsh winters of 1985 and 1986. Lawns and flowerbeds. The Museum houses frescoes by J.H. Fragonard and his son Alexandre. Rose Festival in May.

MENTON

Botanic Gardens of Val Rahmeh
Avenue Saint Jacques. National Museum of Natural History. Open every day except Tuesday from 10am to noon and from 2pm to 4pm (5pm from 1 February to 30 April), and from 3pm to 6pm from 1 May to 30 September. Tel: 93 35 86 72. 1 hectare/2.5 acres with 700 species of plants from America, Asia, Australia and New Zealand and includes olive trees, Japanese bamboo, yuccas, mimosa, lotus, papyrus and a wide variety of different plants from sugar cane to tomato trees.

Villa Serena
21 Rue Reine Astrid. By appointment only. Property of the town of Menton since 1947. Victorian-style villa. Collection of 100 palm trees and subtropical plants on a site of 2 hectares/5 acres.

Val Rahmeh, Menton.

Jardin Exotique, Monaco.

PRINCIPALITY OF MONACO

Jardin Exotique
Boulevard du Jardin Exotique. Open every day from 9am to 6pm (7pm from 1 June to 30 September). Tel: 93 30 33 65. 11,500 square metres/13,800 square yards devoted to one of the world's most visited gardens (600,000 visitors a year) and the

most photographed site on the Riviera. Century-old specimens, views of the Principality and the French-Italian shoreline. Created on the initiative of Prince Albert I between 1914 and 1933, the gardens initially housed a collection of succulent plants dating back to 1895. The collection continued to grow and the gardens now contain a vast number of succulents.

NICE

Jardin des Arènes

Place du Monastère de Cimiez. Municipal park. Open every day from 9 am to 5 pm from 1 November to 31 March; 9am to 7pm from 1 April to 31 May; 8am to 8pm from 1 June to 31 August; 3am to 7pm from 1 to 30 September. Admission free.
1 hectare/2.5 acres of terraced land with rose pergolas, flowerbeds, lawns planted with orange, lemon, and mandarin-orange trees.

Parc Floral 'Phoenix'

405 Promenade des Anglais, 06200 Nice. Open every day, from 20 June to 20 August, 10am to 8pm, except Mondays; from 21 August to 30 September, 10am to 6.30pm; from 1 October to 31 March, 10am to 5pm; from 1 April to 20 June, 10am to 6.30pm. Annual closing 4-31 January.
7 hectare/17 acre park and 'Le Diamant Vert', a greenhouse 27 metres/88.5 feet high, with a floor area of 8000 square metres/9570 square yards, whose tropical environment includes an Amazonian forest, cascades and orchids. Outside, Mediterranean and subtropical flora. 40 species of palm trees.

SAINT-JEAN-CAP-FERRAT

Villa Ile de France

Avenue E. de Rothschild. Open every day except Monday from 2pm to 6pm (3pm to 7pm in July and August). Closed throughout November. Tel: 93 01 33 09.
Total 7 hectares/17 acres. French-style park, Spanish, Florentine, Japanese and English-style gardens, rock garden and exotic gardens. In the Spanish garden, around a pond surrounded by pink marble columns, arums, philodendrons, pomegranate trees, papyrus, datura. In the rock garden, Judas trees and camphor trees. Bamboo in the Japanese garden. Roses,

wild irises, palms, yuccas, lotus and waterlilies in the garden and park. Built between 1905 and 1912 for the Baroness Ephrussi de Rothschild, this Venetian palace became the property of the Institute of France in 1934.

Villa Ile de France, Saint-Jean-Cap-Ferrat.

ST REMY

Van Gogh's Walk

For information contact: the Office of Tourism, St Rémy de Provence, Place Jaurès, 13210 St Rémy de Provence.
Tel: 90 92 05 22.
The picturesque town of St Rémy is where Vincent Van Gogh spent a year while receiving treatment for a psychological disorder in the Cloisters of St Paul, on what is now called the Avenue Vincent Van Gogh. The fields around the Cloister include a well-marked trail leading to gardens and landscapes painted by the artist. The countryside beyond the walls of the Cloister has olive groves and vistas of the Alpilles mountains that are largely unchanged from the time Van Gogh lived there. He painted some 26 canvases in the garden of the Cloister, which is surrounded by a high stone wall and is not open to the public.

THE PAINTINGS

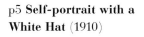

BIBLIOGRAPHY

André, Albert and Elder, Marc *L'Atelier de Renoir* (2 vols) Bernheim-Jeune, Paris, 1931
— *Renoir's Atelier* Alan Wofsy Fine Arts, San Francisco, 1989

Arts Council of Great Britain *Renoir* exhibition catalogue by John House *et al*, London 1985; Abrams, New York, 1985

Broadskaya, Natalia *Auguste Renoir* Collets UK, Northants, 1984

Galérie Durand-Ruel *Renoir, Collection Maurice Gangnat* Paris, 1955, catalogue

Gaunt, William *Renoir* Phaidon, Oxford, 1982

Harris, Frank *Contemporary Portraits* Brentano, New York, 1920; G. Richards, London, 1924

Pach, Walter *Pierre-Auguste Renoir* Thames & Hudson, London, 1984
— *Renoir* Abrams, New York, 1983

Peppiatt, Michael *Architectural Digest* Knapp Communications, Los Angeles, California, 1990

Renoir, Jean *Renoir, My Father* Collins Fontana, London, 1965

Rivière, Georges *Renoir et Ses Amis* H. Floury, Paris, 1921

Rouart, Denis *Renoir* Skira, Geneva, 1954
— *The Unknown Degas and Renoir in the National Museum of Belgrade* McGraw-Hill, London and New York, 1964
— *Renoir* Rizzoli International, New York, 1985; Weidenfeld & Nicolson, London, 1985

Salmon, André *La Vie Passionnée de Modigliani* Intercontinentale du Livre, Verviers and Paris, 1957

Smith, Alan H. *The Brenthurst Gardens* The Brenthurst Press, Houghton, South Africa, 1988

Taylor, Basil (ed.) *The Impressionists and Their World* Phoenix House, London, 1953

Vollard, Ambroise *Recollections of a Picture Dealer* trans V.M. Macdonald, Constable, London, 1936; Little-Brown, Boston 1936
— *En Ecoutant Cézanne, Degas, Renoir* B. Grasset, Paris, 1938
— *Renoir's Paintings, Pastels and Drawings* Alan Wofsy Fine Arts, San Francisco, 1989

Wadley, Nicholas (ed.) *Renoir: A Retrospective* H.L. Levin, New York, 1987

Wheldon, Keith *Renoir and his Art* Hamlyn, London, 1975

INDEX

◆

AUTHOR'S ACKNOWLEDGMENTS

◆

My list of thanks covers four great gardening nations: France, Great Britain, Japan and the United States of America.

First, in France, a special thank you to Michel Colas, director of tourism for the Côte d'Azur, both for inviting me to the South of France to photograph French gardens, and for his and his wife Marie's hospitality. It was also Michel who suggested the idea for a book about Renoir's life at Les Collettes when he saw my enthusiasm for the garden there, and who undertook a great deal of research for the book, as well as serving as interpreter.

I spent many memorable hours with Jacques Renoir and his wife, Anne, both at Les Collettes and at dinner discussions in Nice. Jacques looks like his famous great-grandfather and he is extremely knowledgeable about the history of Les Collettes. He speaks with such insight into Renoir's lifestyle during those years and is intimately involved in the restoration of the property and raising funds for its continued care. Thanks also to the conservator of museums for the City of Cagnes, Georges Dussaule, and to the caretakers of Les Collettes, René and Gisèle Nicolaï, for providing anecdotes and archive pictures for the book. Though we have not yet met, the Mayor of Cagnes, Mme Suzanne Sauvaigo, also deserves special recognition for helping to ensure the survival of Les Collettes.

In England, thanks should go to O. D. Gallagher who taught me to write; Harry Smith who taught me to photograph plants and gardens and my publisher Frances Lincoln. Our first meeting was at Les Collettes, where we enjoyed a tour of the house and garden and later brainstormed ideas for the book over lunch in a delightful café at the Château Grimaldi.

In the United States, Carolyn Heath was a big inspiration, providing for my physical and emotional welfare as I spent long hours assembling my material. Kathy Nelson, my administrative assistant, and Wendy Fields, my grounds supervisor at Cedaridge Farm, held the fort during my travels and helped with typing and picture selection.

Finally, thanks to David Burpee, the American seedsman, and Hiroshi Makita, the Japanese landscape designer, who both taught me about gardens; and to my mother for her words of wisdom whenever I needed advice.

Right Venus Victrix

Publisher's Acknowledgments

The publishers would like to thank the following for their help in producing this book: Penny David, Tim Foster, Elfreda Powell, Paul Reid, Tony Lord, Georges Dussaule, Kwong Fat, Katy Foskew, Georgina Harris, Lucy Rix, and Sue Gladstone for the index.

Editor *Diana Loxley*
Design *Roger Walton Studio*
Picture research *Sue Gladstone*
Illustrator *Mitch Stuart*
Production *Adela Cory*
Picture Editor *Anne Fraser*
Art Director *Caroline Hillier*
Editorial Director *Erica Hunningher*

Photographic Acknowledgments

(*a*=above *b*=below *l*=left *r*=right)

All colour photography © Derek Fell

The Publishers have made every effort to contact all holders of copyright works. All copyright-holders we have been unable to reach are invited to contact the Publishers so that a full acknowledgment may be given in subsequent editions.

For permission to reproduce the paintings and photographs in this book and for supplying photographs, the Publishers thank:
The Bridgeman Art Library: p15, p57
The Brooklyn Museum, New York: p67
The Carnegie Museum of Art, Pittsburgh: p49
Christie's Colour Library: p25, p40, p52, p55, p69, p83, p87, p95, p96
Museum of Fine Arts, Boston: p19
The National Gallery, London: p45
National Gallery of Art, Washington: p32
Photographie Durand-Ruel, Paris: p20*a*, p21*r*, p43*b* (Collection Jacqueline Besson), p45*l*, p74*a*, p93*b*, p94*b*, p97, p107*a*, p108*l*, p108*r*
Photo Serge, Cagnes-sur-Mer: p1, p43*a*
Service de Presse, Mairie de Cagnes-sur-Mer: p27 and back jacket, p42, p44, p79, p91
Sotheby's Inc., New York, © 1988: p80

Path edged with a mass of wild flowers including blue anchusa, yellow mustard and red poppies.